"Queenie"

Letters from an Australian Army Nurse 1915-1917

Researched and edited by Pat Richardson and Anne Skinner

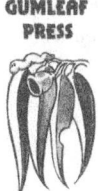

GUMLEAF PRESS

Queenie: Letters from an Australian Army Nurse, 1915-1917

First published in 2012
This edition published by Gumleaf Press

Technical assistance from Paper Horse Design & Publishing
www.paperhorsedesign.com.au

A copy of this publication can be found in the National Library of Australia

ISBN 9780646558356 (pbk.)
ISBN 9780646967042 (ebk.)

The authors wish to acknowledge the support of the Australian Government Department of Veterans' Affairs, which provided a grant to assist publication under the Australian Government's Commemorations program, 'Saluting Their Service'.

"Queenie"

Letters from an Australian Army Nurse

1915-1917

The letters were written from Egypt, France and England to her mother and younger brothers in Townsville, North Queensland.

The letters were found and transcribed by Pat Richardson, Nambucca Heads, N.S.W. Australia.

Researched and edited by Pat Richardson and Anne Skinner
Chapter 1 and additional material by Anne Skinner.

Ms Pat Richardson
PO Box 380
Nambucca Heads NSW 2448
Ph. 02 6568 6239
Email: pat.richardson@westnet.com.au

Anne Skinner
Kalgoorlie WA 6430
Email: sannets@gmail.com
Covers designed by Anne Skinner

Contents

The Avenell Family, 1912

Violet Marian Avenell married Robert Kenneth Waugh in Bowen Queensland, April 8, 1912. Back row (from left): Roley Avenell, (Queenie's oldest brother, who died not long after this with valvular heart disease, aged 27); an unknown person; William Hamilton.

Middle row (from left): Queenie's father, Richard Goodall Avenell, Headmaster of Bowen Boys State School, drowned in the Bowen Baths 1914; Queenie's mother, Matilda Jane Avenell, née Lee who died in Sydney 1940, aged 78; Ivy Walker, the Bridegroom Robert Kenneth Waugh; Bride Violet Marian Avenell, known as 'Dolly'; Edith Florence Avenell, always known as 'Queenie; Gladys Waugh; Denis Walker. Front row: Queenie's younger brothers Bob, Len and Jim Avenell.

Sisters Queenie and Dolly Avenell in about 1906. The photograph was taken in Clermont or Bowen.

Restored by Colleen Myhill, Nambucca

Foreword

By Rosslyn Héro

Finding Queenie's letters was a revelation to my brother and me and also to my cousin, Patricia Richardson (née Avenell). It was Pat who found them at the bottom of her mother's glory box, and then had them arranged, typeset, copied and had the photos added.

My mother died when I was twelve and my brother Dick was ten and neither she nor my father ever talked about the war. From the letters, one can see she was a hard working nursing sister, very patriotic, very loving and financially supportive to her mother back home, and very bright and flirtatious on her days off, especially, in England after her ordeal in France. In those days the nurses were only allowed to go out with the officers.

While nursing at the Army hospital at Kangaroo Point in Brisbane in late September, 1918, Queenie was struck down with acute ptomaine poisoning, where she was saved from death by my father, Dr. Harvey Walsh. She married him in 1919. Queenie died very young at forty-six, from an aneurism of the brain, the day she reached A grade in golf.

I hope the letters will help to recall the devotion to duty of the era and the fascinating account of the little daily things which made up their lives.

Rosslyn Héro (née Walsh),
Queenie's daughter,
Ekebin, Brisbane,
Queensland, Australia.

Introduction

By Pat Richardson

This collection of letters and photos has been collated by me so that they won't be lost, as so much of what women have done in the past has been forgotten.

My aunt, Edith Florence Avenell, known as "Queenie", was a woman of great vitality and was remembered by all who knew her with much respect and love. She died quite suddenly aged only forty-six years in Brisbane in 1936. My father said she was the youngest Matron from Queensland to enlist in the Australian Army Nursing Service in the First World War. She was twenty-five years old. She subsequently served in Egypt, France and England between 1915 and 1917.

I found the letters in 1981 in my mother's glory box; they were written by Queenie to her mother, Matilda Jane Avenell, née Lee, and her two little brothers still at home, Len and Bob. (Len was my late father and he was eleven years old when these letters commenced in 1915). They had moved to Townsville in North Queensland after my grandfather, Richard Goodall Avenell, Headmaster of Bowen Boys State School, drowned in the Bowen Baths in 1914.

The sentiments expressed through the letters about the war are very patriotic and perhaps sound war-like. However, Queenie was a typical first generation Australian of English descent with family ties still very close in England. The family on the maternal side had been members of the British Army for generations and her grandfather, Robert Henry, Sergeant Major "Harry" Lee, had served as a pharmacist with Florence Nightingale in the Crimean War and then he served in the Abyssinian War.

There is much mention through the letters about money, or lack of it. Mrs Avenell had been widowed in 1914 and left penniless with two small boys to bring up. The sole breadwinner of the family at the time of the letters was my Uncle Jim Avenell, who was nineteen years old, and was a clerk in the Union Bank at Townsville.

In 1883 the Avenells had been selected from five hundred applicants in England to be schoolteachers to the Colony of Queensland and were posted to the Two Mile School just north of Gympie, in south-east Queensland. Mrs Avenell was also required to teach sewing and cooking. She was never paid, of course. She was a qualified teacher in England, at Saint Margaret's, Westminster. She also bore ten children.

I would like to acknowledge the late Miss Ailsa Dawson M.B.E. of Gympie for her letters and correspondence with me regarding the family. I would also like to acknowledge my mother, 'Birdie' Mavis Avenell of Allambie Heights, for her bower bird instincts in looking after the letters and photos through countless moves in the bank. I would like to thank my cousin, Rosslyn Héro, née Walsh, of Brisbane for lending me her late mother's album containing photos of Queenie during the war, and also the Anzac Cove photos mentioned in the letters.

Since my discovery of these letters, many years have passed. My mother 'Birdie' and also Miss Dawson have died, and in early 2007, I was joined by then-Gympie journalist Anne Skinner in undertaking more research on the letters and the various people mentioned in them to fill out Queenie's life and times. While she was working at *The Gympie Times*, Anne came upon a copy of the original manuscript of the letters I had given to Miss Dawson and which were in her papers in the town's archives. Miss Dawson was a great local Gympie historian, living at The Two Mile and Anne was doing an Anzac supplement for *The Gympie Times* on local men and women who had served in the First World War. Anne, who has discovered many wonderful photos and data, mainly from the Australian War Memorial and the National Archives of Australia, moved to Kalgoorlie, Western Australia, in 2008 to take up the position of deputy editor, and later editor, of the *Kalgoorlie Miner*. I was also able to do research in London on the Southall Amputee Hospital in October 2008, and would like to thank Dr. Oates, the local historian at the Ealing Broadway Library, for finding wonderful photos for me to select from and sending copies of them to me by email.

During this long gap of years, the collection of letters has been typed out twice, originally in 1983 by The Printery at Nambucca Heads, for which I thank them, and again in 2007 by Ms Simpson of Taylors Arm. The original manuscript was done on cards, which are no longer able to be read, and the new version is in Word, which makes it much more flexible to work with. In early 2011, The Printery at Nambucca Heads once more undertook the typesetting, to include the photos and the extra research Anne and I have done in the past few years. We were then able to submit the manuscript to the Department of Veterans Affairs for a "Saluting Their Service" grant. The grants are being given to commemorate the Centenary of Anzac in 2015 and, happily, we were successful in our application.

When I moved to live in Sydney in 1984, I endeavoured to get the manuscript of letters published, but although it looked likely a couple of times, it failed to go ahead. Then I began a BA degree at the University of Technology, in 1985, (as the oldest uni student in Sydney!). During this time, I gave two talks on the letters at history conferences of the Australian War Memorial. I also gave the original letters to the Australian War Memorial on open access, accompanied by a copy of the original typeset manuscript, which made the letters much easier for people to read and, over the years, other authors have quoted from the letters in their books on Australia's Army nurses, including, 'The Forgotten Women' by Gwen Robinson, 'Guns and Brooches', by Jan Bassett, and 'Queensland Nurses, Boer War to Vietnam' by Dr. Rupert Goodman.

I produced a radio show of the letters, which were read by Lee Abernethy of Nambucca Heads, and which was broadcast on 2SER-FM in November, 1986, as part of my Radio Degree and later on 2RRR-FM and 2NVR-FM. I had the photos restored over the years and they have also been used by many other authors, and also used in a display at Macquarie University on 'Women at War'. The university very kindly restored some of the photos. Freemans Studios, Sydney restored some, and Zenys Photographic Studio, Nambucca Heads.

In 1990 and 1991 I wrote and self-published two books of stories, which I had read over 2SER- FM's New Horizons program each week from 1987 to 1989. Many of the stories were slightly fictionalised, but based on my life. The books were called 'Belle the Bushie' and 'Belle on a Broomstick'. 'Belle the Bushie' won the 1991 Hilarie Lindsay Award from the N.S.W. Women Writers Society. I included a chapter in 'Belle on a Broomstick' on Queenie and included the famous photo of her sitting in the snow at the Australian Auxiliary Hospital for Amputees at Southall with all the young men around her; they had been having a snow fight and most of them had at least one limb missing.

I have also given many talks through the years on the letters and continue to do so. In 1992 I moved back to Nambucca Heads and, in between my many activities, I still get back to working on the letters and keeping up emailing with various relatives, who add a bit more to the story and sometimes a correction or two. Thank you to my second cousin Les Whelan of Brisbane for one surname corrected, and other items of family history, also to June Matthews of Nambucca Heads and Ros Lee of Currumbin for their valuable research.

When I first found the letters, World War One had dropped out of people's consciousness to a great extent, and Anzac Days were in the doldrums. However, there has been a great re-awakening of interest these past ten years, as shown by the huge crowds now at Anzac Cove in Turkey each Anzac Day. And now the Western Front in France is seeing renewed interest in the battles fought there, which actually claimed many more Australian and New Zealand lives than did Gallipoli.

Also, while overseas in October 2008, I took the opportunity to visit the grave of Queenie's cousin, Major Harry William Lee, who was killed in action on 20th March, 1917, in France and is buried at Achiet-Le-Grand War Cemetery near Arras. He was twenty-four years old. As I wrote in the Visitors' Book, "It's a cold old place for a Queensland boy to lie." No disrespect to the Commonwealth War Graves Commission, as the graves and the grounds are in pristine condition, but it was a late autumn morning, the sun was missing and the fields around were all tilled and bare.

The World War One tour I went on for four days and three nights took me to many places of interest to Australians. It was an excellent tour, based in Flanders, near Ypres and the words Fromelles, Polygon Wood, Villers Brettonneux and Pheasant Wood now have greater meaning for me. Whole families of Australians travelling overseas, including children, joined our tour.

The human waste of that war beggars the mind. What a loss to Australia were all those bright young men – sixty thousand of them killed in action – and those nurses who also died on active duty. In the 1911 census, Australia's population was only a little under four and a half million. In all, two thousand, one hundred and thirty-nine nurses served abroad, four hundred and twenty-three served in Military Hospitals here in Australia, twenty-nine died in overseas service, and three hundred and eighty-five were decorated for their coolness and devotion to duty under fire. They served in places as diverse as India, Burma, the Persian Gulf, Palestine, Lemnos, Egypt, Salonika, Italy, Greece, France, England, New Guinea and Vladivostok in Russia.

In 2009 I received a delightful surprise when a manuscript of the letters of Queenie's cousin, Major Harry William 'Willie' Lee, appeared in my email inbox, so items from these will be used here and photos of Willie can now be included in the story. I would like to thank Valmai Arnold, née Lee, of Port Macquarie and Dick Monks, of Naremburn, for permission to use items from the Lee letters. If readers get a bit muddled by all the Harry, Bill and Willie Lees, I will endeavour to indicate which ones they are by their army rank: the original 'Harry', Robert Henry, was a Sergeant Major and pharmacist at Crimea with Florence Nightingale; Colonel Harry Lee, his son, a school headmaster at Maryborough, Queensland, commanded the Queensland 9th Battalion at the landing at Gallipoli; and his son, Major Harry William Lee, 'Willie' or 'Bill' Lee, served at Gallipoli and was killed in France in 1917. The Lees always called him 'Bill' and the Avenells always called him 'Willie'. I was fortunate when I was first transcribing Queenie's letters to have known her brothers, my uncles, Andy and Jim, and, as her way of expressing things was similar to theirs, it was easy to read them and type away.

I hope you will enjoy reading these letters and I feel it is my privilege and honour to have found them and preserved them for the coming generations of young Australians to know their history.

Thank you to the Department of Veterans Affairs for its confidence in our project, and thank you to Bookpal of Brisbane, whose staff are guiding this manuscript through to its completion as an e-book and printed book on demand.

Pat Richardson, née Avenell.
Nambucca Heads.
N.S.W., Australia,
April, 2012.

Chapter 1: Leaving Home

The Townsville docks were crowded with people, piles of baggage and freight, trucks, wagons and horses. It was the beginning of May, 1915, and it seemed as if the whole town had turned out to farewell the ship moored at the Jetty Wharf on Townsville Harbour's Eastern Breakwater. Dock workers swung gantries loaded with heavy luggage, bales and crates aboard the coastal steamer *SS Bombala* as the passengers climbed the canvas-clad gangplank. Family groups, clusters of men and women and a few soldiers crowded the decks, and the last visitors stepped ashore as the ship's horn blasted its mournful warning of imminent departure.

Among the passengers was a young woman travelling alone on the first leg of a journey into an unknown future. Experienced hospital nurse and matron, Edith Florence Avenell, known to her family and friends as Queenie, had volunteered to serve her country in what was to become known as the World War or the Great War and, later – the sobriquet born of the desperate hopes of those who witnessed its devastation – the War To End All Wars.

Who else was on that passenger list? They were mostly men: businessmen or mine owners who may have been travelling to clinch deals in Brisbane, Sydney or Melbourne; young men heading south in the hope of finding work, or to enlist in the war raging in far-off Europe and, more recently, a place most of them had never have heard of before: the Dardanelles. At least one family was aboard, perhaps on the first leg of a holiday, while three women were journeying south with their children. One of several women travelling alone on the *Bombala,* Queenie enlisted the day after the combined forces of Australians and New Zealanders in their brand new ANZAC alliance stormed the beaches of Gallipoli, although she would not have been aware of it as she signed her name and the date – April 26, 1915 – to her attestation paper.

By the time Sister Queenie Avenell boarded the *SS Bombala,* all Australia knew that the two young nations of the West had gone head to head with the old empire of the East, the Ottoman Empire, and were now fighting against not only Germany but her newest ally. On April 29, 1915, the Sydney Morning Herald carried a very brief report on the landings at Gaba Tepe and Cape Helles by Australian, New Zealand, British and French forces, but it wasn't until about two weeks after the attack that fuller details were reported in Australian newspapers. So as she watched the gangplank being raised and the *SS Bombala* made ready to sail, Queenie would have been aware that another front in the war had opened up. Not that it made any difference to her resolve to do her bit – she was willing to go wherever she was needed to nurse Australian soldiers.

Born in the south-east Queensland gold mining town of Gympie, Edith Florence Avenell was raised with her brothers and elder sister Violet – known by the nickname of Dolly – at the Two Mile, a small settlement just north of the town, where her parents, Matilda and Richard Avenell, were school teachers. They had been recruited in England in 1883 from five hundred applicants to teach in the young colony of Queensland. Mrs Avenell was also required to teach sewing and cooking; despite being a qualified teacher, she was never paid for this work.

When Queenie was a baby, her father was transferred to the state's capital city, Brisbane, as headmaster of the Ashgrove State School, where she was to complete most of her schooling. About 1904, when Queenie was around fourteen years old, her father was transferred to Clermont in central Queensland; he was later transferred again, to the north Queensland town of Bowen. When she left school, Queenie completed her nursing training at the Mackay General Hospital before being posted to several small north Queensland towns where, over the next few years, she was to rise in her chosen profession: she held the position of head nurse at Chillagoe Hospital and was later appointed matron of the Bowen Hospital – believed to be the youngest matron thus far to serve in a Queensland hospital.

By the outbreak of war in August 1914, Queenie was the busy matron of the Innisfail Hospital and, as Australians rushed to enlist to fight for King and Empire, she would have been one of the many nurses frustrated by the slow response of the Australian Army Nursing Service to the war. The Army Nursing Reserve was called up soon after war was declared, but the authorities considered no more nurses would be required and it was decided that male orderlies would mostly be used to nurse the troops. However, as the fighting on the Western Front stalled into a bloody turmoil of injured and dying soldiers for little gain on either side, the authorities in Australia and Britain realised they needed more skilled medical staff, and civilian nurses were encouraged to enlist.

So Queenie resigned her position, handed over her hospital files and said goodbye to the many friends she had made in her short time in the small north Queensland town. Just before leaving Innisfail, she was farewelled at a reception held at the residence of the local doctor, Dr Willis. The Townsville Daily Bulletin's Innisfail correspondent introduced the account of the evening with the words: "It is when we are about to lose our friends that we most appreciate them" and goes on to report:

"On Saturday evening, the hospital staff and a number of Matron Avenell's friends gathered at the residence of Dr Willis to bid farewell to Matron Avenell and to make a presentation, as some slight token of the esteem in which she is held. Dr Willis was absent in Cairns and unfortunately, Dr Maloney, who was to have made the presentation, was called out professionally at the last moment. On behalf of those present, Mr Siddey presented Miss Avenell with a beautiful watch bangle, also a valuable dressing case, assuring Miss Avenell that she took away the best wishes of all with whom she had come into contact, and on every side could be heard the wish expressed that when she had fulfilled her noble office at the front, she would return to Innisfail. Such expressions speak volumes for Miss Avenell's popularity, when we consider she is practically a newcomer to Innisfail. Miss Avenell feelingly thanked those present, not only for the gifts which she would always treasure, but also for the kindness always shown to her by the Innisfail people. Mrs Willis made an admirable hostess."

Then it was time to say goodbye to her beloved family. Queenie was very close to her mother, perhaps even more so after the tragic death the previous year of her father, who had drowned in the Bowen swimming baths. Packing up her possessions and her farewell gifts, she travelled from Innisfail to Cairns, most likely by train, and boarded the *SS Kuranda* for the trip south to Townsville, arriving on Friday, 23rd April. The *Townsville Daily Bulletin* of 24th April, 1915, carried the following gossip piece: "Miss Queenie Avenell, Matron of the Innisfail Hospital, has received orders to proceed to the front as a staff nurse. She arrived on Friday to bid farewell to her mother, Mrs Avenell, 'Bon Abri', Strand, and her sisters *(sic: she had only one sister),* before leaving for Brisbane". (Despite that report, she had yet to complete her attestation papers for military nursing service.)

Queenie spent about a week with her mother, married sister Dolly and three younger brothers in Townsville before boarding the *SS Bombala,* one of the passenger and freight steamers that plied the coast of Queensland. As the ship pulled slowly away from the dock, she would have joined scores of other passengers at the railings, craning her neck for a last glimpse of her family below as the busy, puffing tugs edged the vessel away from the wharf. Who knew when she would see them – or Australia – again?

Throughout the next few years of her service overseas, Queenie's only link with home were the letters she exchanged with her mother and other family members. Her letters, reproduced in full in this book, vividly describe the places she sees, the people she meets and her experiences nursing men shattered by the war, and provide an intriguing insight into the times. The letters sketch an image of an independent, modern young woman with a strong personality and opinions, plenty of common sense and a well-developed sense of humour. She worked hard, upheld high professional standards and was proud of her family and her country. Like her sisters in uniform, Queenie was raised to revere King and Empire and her letters home frequently affirmed her support for the war, even though she deplores its effects on "the boys" and grieves for the friends who, over the next four years, were lost to bullets, gas, disease and even suicide.

And like most women throughout the ages, she also loved pretty things and smart clothes; she enjoyed the theatre, flirting with men and a good party! At five feet, six inches (almost one hundred and sixty-eight centimetres) Queenie was tall for the era, with brown hair and striking dark eyes. Slender and attractive, she had a ready smile and a knack of connecting with others – the letters she wrote to her mother often refer to her many friends among the other nurses and the frequent invitations to social outings by the officers. When she had time off from her hospital ward duties in Egypt and England she enjoyed attending dinners, picnics and the theatre on the arm of one admirer or another and was, throughout the war, to receive several marriage proposals.

All this was ahead of Queenie on that day in the May of 1915, as the *Bombala's* captain set a southerly course for Brisbane. Outside Townsville harbour, a brisk north Queensland breeze whipped the tops of the waves into foamy whitecaps. Despite being in the shelter of the Great Barrier Reef, the vessel pitched and rolled in the choppy seas and some of the passengers were soon too seasick to eat their first shipboard meal. Queenie was one of them, as she writes in a letter to her mother on 7th May, a few days after the ship docked in Brisbane: "…the trip down was very choppy and I was seasick once, felt squeamish all the way through."

Once in Brisbane, the serious business of getting ready for army nursing service began. There were uniform fittings at Finney's, then Brisbane's premier dressmaking establishment, inoculations against typhoid, luggage to purchase and banking arrangements to send her mother a monthly allotment from her wages. Throughout the war, Queenie was to send the family the bulk of her earnings as well as gifts from wherever she was posted; she was of a generation which took seriously the support of family.

In May 1915 bulletins about the war were grim: news of the wounded from the Gallipoli landing was filtering into the newspapers and this first letter to her mother reflects the prevailing gloom in Australia. She is anxious about her uncle, Colonel Harry Lee, who commanded the Queensland 9th Battalion, among the first ashore at Gallipoli, and her cousin, Major Will Lee, also known as Billy Lee, who served at Gallipoli but was to be killed in action later in France: "The war news is awful, and everybody looks glum and sad, and talks of nothing else but the casualties, waiting for the fresh news editions," she writes on 7th May. "Grandad says he won't go up to you, until he hears about Uncle Harry and Will. We expect to hear they are killed any day. Robertson, Uncle's Adjutant, is injured." Major James Campbell Robertson of Toowoomba was injured in the landing at Gallipoli. He later commanded the 9th Battalion and rose to the rank of Brigadier General.

"Oh dear, tonight's news is terrible," the letter continues. "The Australians are so brave. What a grand work is before us. We shall be at the hospitals at Heliopolis and the Dardanelles, nursing our own boys." Nursing their own boys was the goal of every Australian nurse and many an Australian soldier was to write home saying they felt immediately better when they heard the comforting voices of "their" girls at their bedsides.

After travelling by train from Brisbane to Sydney, Queenie embarks from Sydney on 15th May with a group of other nurses, all reinforcements for No. 1 Australian General Hospital, and writes: "The French sailors were singing the Marsellaise, and the orderlies, the Australian national songs. It was glorious and far better then I ever thought it could be." Aboard the P&O passenger liner *Mooltan*, which had been requisitioned for war transport, was a mixture of nurses, military reinforcements and civilian passengers heading for England or Egypt. Some of them were the wives of officers who were to set up house in either place for their husbands to come home to. For the newly-appointed military nurses, life aboard ship is fun, but there is work to be done too – Queenie mentions a lecture on the life of Florence Nightingale and the sisters have lectures and drills every day. But the P&O passenger liner also has entertainment aboard and the nurses and troops enjoy musical interludes between their training sessions.

"Miss Irene Brown, the actress, is playing the piano while I am writing. She can play, too, but I don't like her at all. She is so conceited and ugly," Queenie writes candidly on 30th May. "We are all having a glorious time. I cannot tell you any of our movements as our letters are strictly censored. I am keeping a diary, though, so you can see it on my return." Unfortunately, that diary was lost decades ago as neither Queenie's niece Pat Richardson nor her daughter Rosslyn Héro have ever seen it. "There is a crowd on board," she writes. "And we have a sports club, games and dances. It is an experience for me and I thank God I became a nurse, otherwise I should never have got this chance. We had a dance last night. I had every one and all the dances are so different, especially ragtime. I even ragged, never did it in my life before either."

The ship traces the southern coastline of Australia, docking at Melbourne and Adelaide, and then Fremantle, taking aboard more soldiers and military equipment as well as civilian passengers. As she sees the shores of Western Australia fading into the distance, Queenie feels the first real pangs of homesickness: "I realised my leave-taking, more than anytime, at Fremantle. Had a long look at dear old Australia," she writes on 27th May. "We are not to give any information in numbers or names of ports, so it will be very hard to write letters. However, you know our next port of call, and we are all looking forward to seeing it and having a rickshaw ride." The next port of call is Colombo, then Bombay before the *Mooltan* navigates the Suez Canal and the nurses and soldiers disembark for the six hour train trip to Cairo, where Queenie and her colleagues immediately begin nursing Gallipoli wounded in one of the military hospitals, a converted palace: "I have thirty-six men to look after and there are dozens of dressings to be done. Really, our feet are simply dreadful by the end of the day. We all rub methylated spirit on them."

For the next few months, her letters are full of the sights, sounds – and smells – of Egypt, and descriptions of hospital life in the converted Sultan Ibrahim Palace at Heliopolis, where soldiers are housed in a giant ward created from the ballroom. She describes the hospital as: "a beautiful building, a real harem too… but we haven't any time to admire the rooms, and it makes you terribly tired just walking round half one storey." Of the city she pens: "Cairo is very interesting. I would never get tired of looking and seeing all there is – but dear old Australia for me every time." Queenie is later to serve in the hospital created from the Luna Park amusement centre, where the ice rink has been drained and turned into a ward. During a time when any available large building is being requisitioned as ward space, she is also to work in hospitals converted from the grand Ghezireh Hotel and the Mena House Hotel.

She reports having "… two hundred in the ward, Typhoid, Pneumonia and Dysentery, all back from the Dardanelles". But despite sore feet and long hours, Queenie makes the most of her time off. She is attractive and single and there is no shortage of officers eager to take her out to see the sights of Cairo. "I enjoyed myself immensely yesterday," she writes on 22nd June. "Had lunch at the Grand Continental and then we took a Gharry *(horse-drawn carriage)* all round the bazaars, visited some mosques and the Egyptian University, which has three thousand students, and the tombs of the Caliphs… It was all very interesting." Egypt is an entrancingly new experience and she is drawn to the atmosphere of Cairo where people "eat out on the streets" – her first sight of outdoor cafes, unknown in country Queensland and even in Brisbane until many decades later.

Queenie's letters are a lively, chatty mixture of news of outings in Cairo and the occasional male conquest, gloomy news of the war, compassionate tales of "her boys" on the ward and a hotch-potch of the sort of rumour and speculation that were the conversational meat and drink of Cairo dinner tables: "One can't believe a thing over here. There are such a lot of yarns going around. We don't hear any news here at all, except from the boys themselves and they can only tell you little of where they are," she writes to her mother. "There are some marvellous escapes really. Bullets and shrapnel flying through them and just above their hearts. One man in my ward had a bullet go through his mouth out of his neck and again in and out of his shoulder. He is going back to the Dardanelles later. I am collecting some great snaps. Those I sent you last week are real photos of the Gallipoli Peninsula taken on the spot. The boys told me there were cameras and glasses all along the beach. They had to throw them down."

In 1915, despite the paucity of accurate war news, the ever-renewing flood of wounded and dying are a daily reminder of the unrelenting bloodshed on the other side of the Mediterranean: "We took a shrap (shrapnel) out of a man's throat today. It was as big as a marble. Poor beggars, all their arms and legs with shrapnel wounds; it is a great strain, and it is a good thing we can get a half a day every other day, off-duty," Queenie writes on 22nd June.

Scattered through the letters are her meetings with men she knows from Queensland before the war, who are also known to her family. She writes to them to cheer them up and pass on messages from home: "I got Dr. Taylor's son Waldon in my ward today, heaps of other nice boys too, they have dysentery and influenza. Young Boddington from Mackay is in with us. He has his face knocked about with a shell explosion, a lucky escape. Some haven't any nose and they look awful. Our poor old boys, they do look awful, poor beggars. Such a lot of the boys are suffering from shock and nervous breakdown. They all have nightmares, yelling out and calling their mates. Some of the patients get terribly affected and think they are fighting again. They are all more or less suffering from the severe strain and shock. The ear and eye ward is next to mine and it would make you sick to see the blind young men about twenty and their hair almost white."

The letters often mention the horrific wounds of the soldiers under her care, and the laconic humour some of her patients exhibit probably helped them survive: "One of my patients was hit with shrapnel in five different places, his eye blown out. Left arm blown off and other wounds on the back and body. He is a brave fellow. He says he is not too bad, but he thinks he got more than his share," she writes on 24th August. "I have two hundred and fifty patients, mostly convalescents. Young Fox from Bombardii is one of them. He says poor Edward Williams from 'Burrenbring' was killed right beside him – everybody seems to be having sorrow and losses in their family now."

But she still makes the most of her chance to see the sights of Cairo. Of her first trip to the Pyramids of Giza she writes on 29th June: "Major McLean took Sister Tyson and me out to the Pyramids. They are much bigger than I expected and the drive out is glorious, beautifully made roads all round… we had our photos taken on the camels." And her first lesson in the local language: "Those little Arabs holding the water jugs, scream out immediately the photo is taken for 'backsheesh', meaning 'present' or 'money'; everything is money or piastres. The boys call them 'disasters'." Queenie also runs into two nurses she worked with in Mackay before the war: "Did I tell you I saw Nurse Derrer? She's over at the No. 2 Ghezireh, and Chidgey arrived last week, so Mackay nurses are being well represented."

She describes Cairo's Red Light District, which would have been an unfamiliar concept to a nicely brought up girl from country Queensland in the early 20th century: "There are three places where the officers go at night and meet French, Greek, Italian, and all races of beautiful women," she writes on 6th July. "They drink and dance with them and then if they wish can go back to their flats with them. No ladies ever go near these places, but I believe all the men go there. One place is called the 'Casino'. No privates are allowed. It is a hot place, alright."

Later there is her account of the so-called Battle of the Wazzir, the sacking of the Red Light District by rampaging Australian troops in August 1915: "Cairo is the wickedest place in the world. Fancy, twenty-five thousand bad women in Cairo, all registered, and our troops had a riot this week and burnt down some buildings in the low quarters. For some reason one of the soldiers was tackled while there, so the crowd got into the place. They are not allowed into Cairo now. They had to call out pickets and order all the boys home."

On another occasion, there is a concert for the troops: "We had an orchestra from 2 p.m. till 5 p.m. in the hall at the Palace, weird and charming. I felt I could cry out. Seeing all the boys round me and this beautiful music. I often think I should not go out and enjoy myself, but it wouldn't do me any good to stay at home."

Romance between soldiers and nurses is inevitable in any war and, after telling her mother she has had several proposals of marriage but isn't in love with any of them and "do not believe I ever will be, with any man", she is attracted to an English soldier who is killed at Gallipoli a few weeks later: "Mum, I made such a nice friend, a Lieutenant Cunningham and he was so good and nice to me. He went to the front and I got three letters from him, and this week his pal wrote to say he is killed," she writes on 14th September. "I feel I can't meet any more of them now. He was such a fine fellow. I feel very down in the dumps. We go out and have such gay times before they go off to the front and then we never see them again. It's wicked and I hate the very mention of war. Although we never get away from it; it is with us day and night."

Despite her resolve not to become involved with any more soldiers, it is only a few weeks before Queenie tells her mother about the tall New Zealander serving with the Australian 6th Light Horse, who is being treated for debility and dysentery. Her letters are soon full of the young Sergeant, Rollie Reid, and the talk is of marriage: "Rollie is such a man, Mother… I know you will like him. I wish this old war was over, we could get married and come back to see you together." In another letter she writes: "I am afraid Rollie and I won't be able to get married till we come back, so you will have me stepping out of our little house in our uniforms. Roll and I had a good old talk about it, but anything might happen." Two years later, when Rollie is in the trenches of France, her fears for his safety intensify and she writes: "I wish now we had got married in Egypt, or else never met at all. He is so careless under fire, too."

Christchurch-born Rolland Arthur Reid was farming in Australia when he enlisted in Sydney on September 8, 1914, at the age of twenty-four. But although it was a love affair lasting more than two years, with talk of marriage in several letters, Queenie suddenly stops mentioning Rollie some months before returning to Australia and, intriguingly, there is never any explanation. It is likely she did tell her mother about the end of the affair, and that letter is probably at the bottom of the Indian Ocean. Queenie's daughter Rosslyn, now in her eighties, told me with a twinkle in her eye: "We all wanted to know who Rollie was – but she probably dropped him. She had lots of boyfriends during the war." What we do know of Rollie, who rose to the rank of Lieutenant, is that he survived the war despite severe wounding and, after demobilisation and repatriation to Australia, returned to his native New Zealand, where he later married.

Despite the dangers from German submarines in 1915, which have already sunk several ships, Queenie is keen to go on transport duty to bring the wounded back from Gallipoli. Although she is told to be ready for deployment at any moment, those orders never come, but in November she has orders to return to Australia with the men who are maimed, mad and unfit for service. After precious time catching up with family, Queenie returns to Cairo and, with the Gallipoli campaign over, the army hospitals ready themselves for relocation to France.

If France was a shock to soldiers who thought Gallipoli was the worst that could happen to them, the shockwaves also rippled as far as the hospitals. Queenie and her colleagues thought they had already seen all that war could show them, but they couldn't have been more wrong. As a wet 1916 summer turned into the coldest and wettest autumn and winter France had known in a century, conditions in the trenches became so bad men were frozen into the muck; they drowned in shell holes, their feet rotted, fever and illness were rife and the casualty rate was in the thousands every single day. Living conditions for the nurses close to the front lines were not only damp, freezing and uncomfortable, they were also dangerously close to enemy fire. Rugged up in greatcoats, boots and steel helmets, they nursed in barely heated tent hospitals just behind the lines, trying desperately to deal with the hundreds of wounded and dying men who passed through their hands each day.

Queenie's unit, No. 1 Australian General Hospital, disembarked at Marseilles on 6th April, 1916 but within two weeks she fell ill with pyrexia and was admitted to No. 14 General Hospital at Wimereux. Discharged on 4th May, she was assigned to No. 13 Stationary Hospital in Bolougne. Unfortunately, only two of Queenie's letters from France survive. There are other gaps in the letters too – some would have been lost in ships that went down and, as the surviving letters were passed around Queenie's extended family, others probably became lost in transit.

In May 1916, she writes to her mother from Boulogne: "I don't know how they – the soldiers – live. This place is pretty, but deadly just now. Can't go anywhere and never out at night. In absolute darkness all the time. Last night we got warning for an air raid but it didn't come off. It is very depressing in France. We all get down to zero. I suppose it is living the whole time with war surrounding. Really, Mother, I don't know what will become of it all, I want to get back to Australia the moment it is all over."

But she never forgets the men at the front and writes to her friends as often as she can: "I had letters tonight from Ross Burrell, Jack Earwaker and Mr Newth, all from the firing lines. I sent them cards and they beg of me to write to them. Poor old chaps, I expect they are very lonely." She also takes the time to write letters home for patients who were too maimed, sick or had lost their sight. And she is one of many nurses who compassionately face the task of writing the hardest letters of all – to the wives and mothers of the men who die in her arms.

In her second remaining letter from her six months in France, this time to family friend and army chaplain, Colonel David Garland, she writes: "We had a big convoy in last night – shocking cases. I simply ran for ten solid hours without a stop." Padre Garland, who served in the Middle East and was the first chaplain to hold a service in the Anglican chapel of the Church of the Holy Sepulchre after the Turks were expelled from Jerusalem the following year, mentions in his letter the gossip spreading in Australia about army nurses and soldiers. Their supposed scandalous behaviour has even been discussed in the newspapers.

In her June 8th letter to the Padre, Queenie reacts strongly to the rumours: "Well, I'm sorry to hear such scandal discussed about the sisters. The only sister I knew got sent back was because she married without the C.O's. permission. Otherwise sisters here are having a trying time. Of course it was different in Egypt – we did go out and had a gay time when off duty during the latter part of our stay there, but why shouldn't we? It gave our troops pleasure to be with us and much better for them than down the town with bad company. I think some people are jealous of the sisters being out here with the troops."

In July 1916 Queenie returns to her original unit, No. 1 Australian General Hospital, now housed in unheated tents on the racecourse at Rouen. Severely under-equipped, the nurses struggle to cope with a never-ending stream of convoys bearing the sick and wounded from the battles of the Somme. The constant parade of horrific wounds, the dead and dying soldiers, the pressure of living in bunker-like conditions so close to the front line and the long hours of work take their toll on Queenie: she suffers a breakdown in September and is sent to England for a fortnight's sick leave.

She writes to her mother from a recuperation home for nurses in St Albans: "I am rather bewildered at the comfort around me and can't realise I am away from active service in France yet… perhaps it is the reaction but I have just cried since I came and it is so silly too. You know I never howl, but I am not so bad today. Yesterday after I had a hot bath and got into bed, my meals were brought to me and everybody is so kind, I felt it was really too much for me. The Sisters look dreadfully ill here, and yet it's really only 'run-down'. They call us the 'Paleface' Brigade."

But with typical down-to-earth practicality she goes on to say: "Well, I'm going to try and forget all the horror I've left behind and enjoy myself." And, once she is allowed up, enjoy herself she does. London is an entertainment and shopping paradise after the gloom and terror of France. There are scores of shows and plenty of restaurants to enjoy with friends on leave from the trenches and she takes full advantage of all of it, as she writes: "Three Colonels all look after me. Colonel Dawson took us to the Tower of London, saw the Crown Jewels and all the historic parts, armouries, scaffolds, etc. I also went one morning to Madame Tussaud's. So you see I'm doing the sights."

Queenie may think she has left the worst of the war behind in France, but some of it follows her to England, for in October 1916 she writes from St Albans: "I saw a Zeppelin come down in a mass of flames the night before last, it lit up our room and we rushed out of bed and just saw it in time... The aeroplane that brought it down was near it, and kept throwing out different coloured lights signalling. It was most exciting, all the people cheering and singing. They say the cries of the men were awful as the Zeppelin came down. Some threw themselves out; of course, they were dead and all burnt. Really, isn't it dreadful, they came over here with the intent to murder people and they get so daring and then are killed themselves?"

Queenie is relieved when she is not sent back to the horrors of France and by November she is on light duties at Southall Hospital where she is treating the most visible fallout from the war – amputees; men maimed for life, but still determined to make the most of their lot. "I will tell you all about the experiences I've had," she writes. "Been on duty all day and I have one hundred and fifty-six dressings to do on about thirty one-armed men. Fancy, some don't need dressing every day and all are up walking about. The 'legs' are in the next ward, and they are so funny, show off how they can hop on the one leg and frighten the heart out of me going past them. If you should call, they come on their stumps."

The war saw a great leap forward in medical science. The first experiments with plastic surgery began and the science of amputation and prosthetics became well advanced. Queenie is impressed by the progress: "That is most interesting when a boy has only his hand taken off," she writes on 30th November. "The Doctors can now operate on the wrist and cut the bone in half, making a joint. Of course, the skin has to be cut to get at the bone, but it heals up and yet the bone is separate, then he can use the hand, etc." But her fears for the future of these maimed men face wring her heart: "They are going back to Australia and are all just shattered wrecks really. I am sorry for Australia, for it will be nothing but broken down men after the war."

However, she is inspired by their indomitable spirit: "All my boys are either winged or legs off, shoulders blown away, big head wounds, but nearly all healed up and just little pieces of dead bone keeping them from healing up altogether. They are such fine fellows. Some have only had twelve operations. I believe the new limbs are just wonderful; one boy was given his legs (both artificial), free, as an advert by the American contractor firm, and he can go upstairs, walked a seven mile route march without any sticks or crutches, so if he can do that with two artificial limbs, a one-legged man can be almost normal. We are getting more stumps every day and have now about three hundred without legs and arms... Yesterday a crowd of the boys were out having a snow fight. Crutches everywhere in the snow and only their one leg."

Despite working long shifts – often ten or more hours a day – Queenie and her friends still find time to take their patients on outings: "Last Saturday afternoon another sister and myself took the real 'stumpies' (boys without legs at all) to the cricket match at Uxbridge, our orderlies against the Canadians." Her social calendar is still filled with dinner and theatre engagements, and she has the thrill of a brush with royalty: "I went to a very swagger dinner party the other day at the Langham Hotel and on our way we saw Queen Alexandra step into her carriage from the Queen's Hall. She was present at some Charity Concert. We thought it was a wedding at first with the crowds, but there was a yell of 'The Queen, The Queen' and of course we felt then we were in the presence of Royalty."

Queenie is still in touch with Rollie Reid, now a Lieutenant serving in France, but the romance appears to have waned. She has another admirer in Bert Norris, a Mackay schoolteacher she knew before the war. "I spent Wednesday with Bert Norris," she writes on 20th October. "He is very fond of me, Mum; it's a pity he did not tell me eight years ago, although I have always had an idea."

In early 1917 Queenie's cousin Billie Lee is killed in action in France, bringing the war right into her own family. She is still nursing at Southall, the London hospital for amputees. "I'm very much afraid he is among the list killed," she writes on 12th April. "There might be another Major H.W. Lee, of course, but I suppose it's only too true." Tragically for the family, it is true. Major Harry William Lee was killed in action near Vaulx-Vraucourt on the Somme on 20th March, 1917. He was siting machine gun positions under enemy artillery fire when a shell tore into his body. His comrades rushed him to the Battalion Aid Post but nothing could save him. Billie Lee died of a massive haemorrhage half an hour later, his last words: "Tell them I died gamely". *(For more on Major Lee, see Appendix 2.)*

The following month Queenie and another nurse go on leave to Scotland, before returning to Southall. A gap in the letters of several months follows, then in early October 1917 Queenie arrives back in Brisbane on her second tour of transport duty. The collection of letters ends at this point. Although she expects to return to England, her orders are changed, apparently at the last minute, and she serves in No.6 Australian General Hospital in Brisbane until 1919. On 17th January, Queenie is discharged from the Australian Army Nursing Service after narrowly surviving a life-threatening illness – and she later marries the doctor who saves her life. She was awarded three medals reflecting her military nursing service: the 1914/1915 Star, the British War Medal and the Victory Medal.

Edith Florence Avenell was one of two thousand, one hundred and thirty-nine Australian nurses who enlisted in the Australian Army Nursing Service to serve in Egypt, Lemnos, England, France, Belgium, Greece, Salonika, Palestine, Mesopotamia and India. One hundred and thirty additional Australian nurses served with the Queen Alexandra Imperial Military Nursing Service – they were mostly women who either were in England when war broke out or, impatient to nurse "their boys", travelled independently to England to enlist while the Australian authorities were dithering about letting them enlist. An unknown additional number of nurses served with the Red Cross or travelled to England to join private wartime hospitals which were set up in Europe, such as the Scottish Women's Hospital which was staffed entirely by women and one of the very few hospitals which employed women doctors. Four hundred and twenty-three nurses also served in military hospitals in Australia.

Australian women had gained the right to vote in federal elections more than a decade before, in 1902, and by 1914 the position of women here had never been stronger. In an era when many young women whose families could afford to keep them still remained at home until marriage, nurses in Australia were among the most emancipated women of their time: they realised the value of education, wanted to make their own way in the world and sought financial independence. The hospital Sisters and Matrons who gave up secure jobs for the uncertainties and privations of war service were, like Queenie, mainly young women in their twenties, well trained to the exacting standards of the latest in medical science. They were for the most part at the forefront of their profession: well qualified, hard working and committed to their careers. They were also patriotic to a degree that appears exaggerated in these days, but which in the early part of last century was the norm: patriotism meant simply an honest pride in their country and automatic loyalty to the British Crown.

Many of these attitudes and sentiments, as well as her personal griefs, triumphs and experiences, are reflected in Queenie's letters home, which begin in Chapter 2.

For more on the soldiers and nurses mentioned in this chapter, see Appendix 1.

St George's
Nurse Home
Milton 7. 5. 15

Dearest Mother

I suppose you have my wire by now & know some of my movements. First I must tell you the trip down was very choppy & I was seasick once felt squeamish all the way though. I arrived in Brisbane on the Tuesday 12 m.d. went out to the General Hospital which is the base H. Dr Hardy examined me thoroughly & passed me. Then he inoculated me for Typhoid. I then came out here. ok. stood for Finney's dressmakers for two hours tired & weary then yesterday I had to go again to Finney's for another two hours getting fitted. have to go again tomorrow. Today I went down to see Coley at Redcliffe she has been down 4 weeks. went on the Koopa & just as we were leaving I bumped into Grandad & the Milne's on their way to Bribie too so we talked & talked. Takes two hrs to go to Redcliffe. The war news is awful & everybody looks glum & sad & talk of nothing else but the casualties waiting for the fresh news editions. Grandad says he won't go up

2.

to you until he hears about Uncle Harry & Will. we expect to hear they are killed any day. Robertson Uncles adjutant is injured. oh dear tonight's news is terrible. the Australians are so brave. what a grand work is before us. we shall be at the hospitals at Heliopolis & the Dardanelles. nursing our own boys. I heard Dr Cowton is going up too Mum. he is under Louis Bond. at the naval bridging train. Miss McDonald has just told me to call at the Courier buildings for some money that has been donated to the 25 nurses. that is a blessing. I am getting a coat grey & scarlet out door it has a large cavalier cape, & looks very nice. it is to hand in £4. 4 0 & then our dresses are grey (pale) zepher white aprons. scarlet capes my own caps all this is allowed us at Finney's. I had to buy a cabin trunk & (canvas all leather) costing me £4 altogether that is all so far. of course a lot of smaller items stockings & new pan bonnets singlets etc. it is a great rush & then next Tuesday I go out for a second dose. serum. we are to be vaccinated on

3

board. We are all leaving Brisbane next Thursday 13th 8 am. per rail for Sydney. & then joining the big P & O. "Mooltan" & leaving for Melbourne on the 15th 12 m d. Saturday. There are 800 altogether troops & all so Mother you see it will not be any holiday trip for us but work straight off. I am so glad I am going now that there are so many wounded Australians how about my salary I am going in to get my affairs all fixed up tomorrow see the Area officer etc. I heard my salary is £60 a year. it is a very poor salary but you can draw £3 of it a month Mum. it will be some help. & Grandad is going up to you he will keep mum what he says. however when I get over I may be made a sister & get a higher screw. Miss McDonald the Matron of this home says its a shame. & some one ought to complain but of course no one will. 7 of our 25 nurses are going to England. & they are getting only £40 a year. so we are really better off. I ran over to see Mrs Lillard last night. & she was so upset & sad at losing little Doris.

4

& of course Auntie won't give up Gordon the baby & she feels it very much. I wish you would write to her Mother. she would be pleased. Leonard is getting on well & his business & has got a motor car he gave £80 for it second hand from Sydney & it is a grand one I believe. Well Mum, I must close I am jolly tired. I could write & tell you more. pass this letter on to Doll & Andy. oh I saw Andy he is just the same. said he hadn't heard from you & wondered why. I shall drop you a P.C. from Sydney & my permanent address. Auntie Susie is living in Maryborough & is not coming to Brisbane Heaps of love dear Mum & the boys.
from. Queenie.

This is on my luggage in white paint & red cross.
Edith Avenell.
Australian Army Nursing Service
1st Australian General Hospital
A. I. F.
I am joining nurse Echlin.

Queenie's first letter to her mother, dated 7th May, 1915.

Notes on reading the letters

Italic notes in brackets explain aspects of the text where the editors feel they are needed, or when there is a page missing. Editors' notes in italic script are also found at the end of some chapters. The letters have been separated into chapters based broadly on where Queenie was serving at the time, such as Egypt, France, Australia and Southall, in England.

Research in newspaper archives as well as family memories underpin some of the assumptions made about the manner of her departure and her attitude to life, which was in general positive and practical. In every way, Queenie was a modern young professional woman of her time and this is certain to resonate with her counterparts of today.

Innisfail Hospital, North Queensland, 1914. (Left to right) Cis Warren, Matron Queenie Avenell, Mrs. Willis, Annie Downey, Elizabeth Davis and Hilda Thompson. Before Queenie left Innisfail, the hospital staff gave her a send-off which was reported in the Townsville Daily Bulletin on 4th May, 1915.

Chapter 2: The Letters – Brisbane to Fremantle

St George Nurses Home,
Milton, Brisbane,
Queensland.
7th May, 1915.

Dearest Mother,

I suppose you have my wire by now and know some of my movements. First I must tell you the trip down was very choppy and I was seasick once, felt squeamish all the way through. I arrived in Brisbane on the Tuesday 12 midday went out to the General Hospital which is the base H.Q. Dr. Hardy examined me thoroughly and passed me. Then he inoculated me for typhoid.

I then came out here, oh, stood for Finney's dressmakers for two hours, tired and dreary. Then yesterday I had to go again to Finney's for another two hours, getting fitted. Have to go again tomorrow. Today I went down to see Coley *(Mrs. Rose Cole, Mrs. Avenell's best friend)*, at Redcliffe, she has been down four weeks. Went on the "Koopa" and just as we were leaving I bumped into Grandad *(Sgt Major Harry Lee)* and the Milnes on their way to Bribie too, so we talked and talked, takes two hours to go to Redcliffe.

The war news is awful, and everybody looks glum and sad, and talk of nothing else but the casualties, waiting for the fresh news editions. Grandad says he won't go up to you, until he hears about Uncle Harry and Will. *(Lieutenant Colonel Harry W. Lee, V.D. Commander of the 9th Battalion at the Landing at Gallipoli and his son, Captain Willie H.W. Lee, Transport officer of the 9th Battalion).* We expect to hear they are killed any day. Robertson, Uncle's Adjutant, is injured.

Oh dear, tonight's news is terrible. The Australians are so brave. What a grand work is before us. We shall be at the hospitals at Heliopolis and the Dardanelles, nursing our own boys. I heard Mr. Cowton *(William Matthew Cowton, surveyor, aged thirty-four)* is going with us too, mum. He is under Thos Bond *(Second in Command, RANBT, Lt. Thomas Bond, Accountant, aged fifty)* at the Naval Bridging Train. *(AWM note as below re the Bridging Train).*

Miss McDonald has just told me to call at the Courier buildings for some money that has been donated to the 25 nurses. That is a blessing. I am getting a coat grey and scarlet (out-door), it has a large cavalier cape and looks very nice. It is to travel in, four pounds, four (shillings), and then our dresses are grey (pale) zephyr white aprons, scarlet capes, my own caps – all this is allowed us at Finney's. I had to buy a cabin trunk and (carry-all, leather), costing me four pounds altogether, that is all so far, of course. A lot of smaller items, stockings and a new pair of corsets, singlets, etc.

It is a great rush and then next Tuesday I go out for a second dose of serum. We are to be vaccinated on board. We are all leaving Brisbane next Thursday 13th, 8 a.m. per rail for Sydney and then joining the big P. & O. "Mooltan" and leaving for Melbourne on the 15th at midday on Saturday. There are 800 altogether, troops and all, so Mother, you see it will not be any holiday trip for us but work straight off. I am so glad I am going now that there are so many wounded Australians.

Now, about my salary: I am going in to get my affairs all fixed up tomorrow, see the area officer, etc., I heard my salary is sixty pounds a year, it is a very poor salary, but you can draw three pounds off it a month, Mum. I will be some help and Grandad is going up to you. He will help from what he says. However, when I get over, I may be made a sister and get a higher screw. Miss McDonald, the Matron of this home, says it's a shame, someone ought to complain, but of course, no one will. Seven of our twenty-five nurses are going to England and they are getting only forty pounds a year. So we are really better off.

I ran over to see Iris Sellars last night, and she was so upset and sad at losing little Doris. Of course, Auntie won't give up Gordon the baby, and she feels it very much. I wish you would write to her, Mother, she would be pleased. Leonard is getting on well with his business and has got a motor car. He gave eighty pounds for a second hand one from Sydney and it is a grand one I believe.

Well, Mum, I must close, I am jolly tired. I could write and tell you more. Pass this letter on to Doll and Andy. Oh, I saw Andy, he is just the same. Said he hadn't heard from you and wondered why. I shall drop you a P.C. from Sydney with my permanent address. Auntie Susie *(Colonel Harry Lee's wife, née Heilbronn),* is living in Maryborough and is not coming to Brisbane.

Heaps of love dear Mum and the boys.

From Queenie.

This is on my luggage in white paint and red cross:

Edith Avenell,
Australian Army Nursing Service,
1st Australian General Hospital, A.I.F.

I am joining Nurse Echlin.

Note from the A.W.M. 16/11/2009 re the Royal Australian Naval Bridging Train: A relatively unknown, but highly decorated unit of the Royal Australian Navy in the First World War. An article in 'Sabretache' Vol XXV111 July to Sept. 1987 is entitled 'The Dry Land Sailors, a short history of the Royal Australian Naval Bridging Train 1915-1917" by Greg Swinden. They built bridges and piers and other handy things, including water supplies to the front line, mainly at Suvla Bay under heavy shelling, and also they built Bridges across the Suez Canal, which they had to put up and take down up to six times daily. As they wore Light Horse uniforms, they were rarely recognized as part of the Navy. They disbanded in 1917, many of them joining the Australian Imperial Forces and going on to fight in France.

Queenie, a studio portrait taken before the war.

Telegram from Melbourne to Mrs. Avenell,
Strand, Townsville, May 17, 1915:

Au revoir dear ones. Keep well. Address Heliopolis Palace Hotel, Egypt.

S.S. Mooltan,
17 May, 1915.

Dearest Mother and boys,

We are just entering Port Melbourne. It is such horrible weather too, raining and cold, in fact the trip from Sydney has been very rough. All the time Saturday were able to sit out on the top deck, but not since. The "Mooltan" is a lovely boat. Music room and saloon, our send-off was grand, and such a bright day. Crowds were on the wharf to see someone belonging to them. Mrs Mighell and Nellie O'Donahue came down to see me. I was glad to have someone to see me. I felt sad and wished you were there too. But we all were smiling and laughing.

The sisters' arms were all laden with flowers, made up in all sorts of shapes, horseshoes, red crosses and baskets. Everyone had a ribbon block holding. Oh dear mum, it was pretty! The French sailors were singing the Marsellaise, and the orderlies, the Australian national songs. It was glorious and far better then I ever thought it could be.

We have doctors coming on at all ports, and sisters too. All our letters are censored and we cannot give any numbers or information at all. I am wondering if I shall see Dr. Cowton. He wired me from Brisbane that he would try to see me. My word, the wind is blowing outside. We went to see "The Man Who Stayed At Home" our night in Sydney, it was very good. We had a nice journey in the train coming down, had a parlour car and sleeper. Dr. and Mrs Hoare are on board. Dr. Hoare is going home and Mrs Hoare is staying in Melbourne. Heaps of love dears to you all.

Queenie xxxxxxxxxx

P.S. We had Church yesterday all in uniform of course. My address C/- Heliopolis Palace Hotel, Heliopolis, Egypt.

The Mooltan leaving Melbourne in May, 1915. AWM5001009

Postcard from Adelaide,
20th May, 1915.

Dearest Mum,

This is from the Post Office we are all out seeing the sights etc. All our letters are to be censored from the boat, so we write from here. "Mooltan" stays one day here. Bill gave me a lovely time in Melbourne. Am writing when go back to the boat. Hope you are all well. Am having a glorious time but a bit seasick. Heaps love.

Xxxxxx Queenie.

S.S. Mooltan
20th May, 1915.

Dearest Mum,

We have been out all day seeing Adelaide. I had a glorious time in Melbourne. Bill and I went to "High Jinks" it is a comic opera and we did like it. I sent you a p.c. from the general P.O. this a.m. There are crowds of us on board, doctors, orderlies and sisters.

I got your telegram and hope you are still all well. I have written you from every port so far but you must write to me at Heliopolis Palace, Heliopolis, Egypt. I like this place very much, like Brisbane, but Melbourne is grand. Heaps of love, the gong to clear the gangway has gone. I shall throw this over to someone, and shall write to you tomorrow.

xxxxxx Queenie.

S.S. Mooltan,
22nd May, 1915.

Dearest Mother, and all at home,

I suppose you often wonder where we are and what I am doing. It is just beginning to get bad weather and the "Mooltan" is tossing a good bit. I don't actually get sick, but just a bit off. Have been to every meal so far. We are being treated very well, first class saloon passage for the doctors and sisters, and the troops second; some of them are such nice fellows.

One I was speaking to told me he had just returned from a trip round the world. He is Captain Darley's cousin, and now he is just an ordinary private. Another one's father presented us with a motor car for ambulance work. We arrive Fremantle tomorrow and leave at 6 p.m. A dance is to be held at 8.45 the same evening.

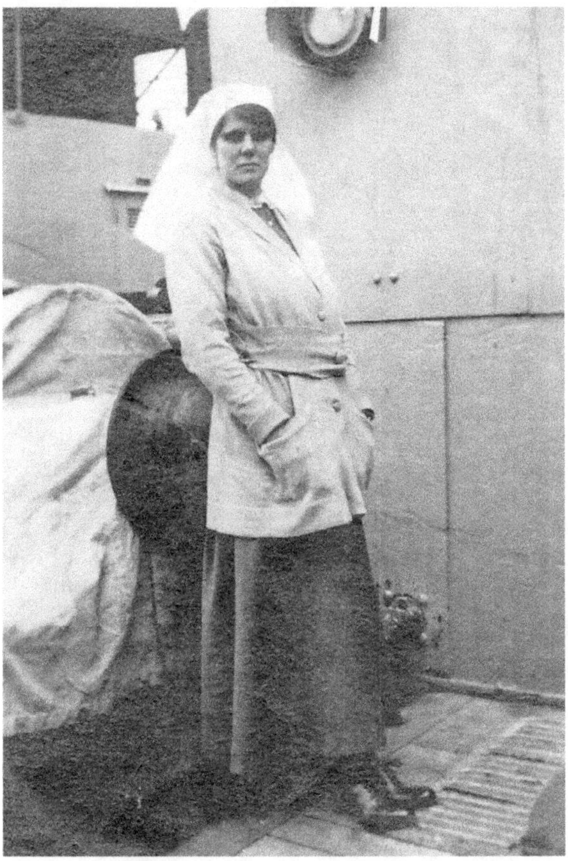

(Letter torn here)

... Took me and St. Kilda dinner at ... And then we went to "High Jinks", back to the boat at midnight just before Matron got in, we were all allowed a late pass of course. The next day we motored all round and through the parks. It was beautiful. I like Melbourne such funny cable cars, different to Sydney.

I told you several of us went to "The Man Who Stayed At Home" in Sydney (Gods). It was splendid. Seven of us got off at Adelaide and saw the Zoo, Museum, Art Gallery and Gardens (I sent you a p.c. from the P.O., it is a nice place too.)

This photograph is from Queenie's own album, taken on her way to Egypt. She is pictured in casual nursing uniform on the Mooltan, May, 1915. Photo restored and enlarged by Zeny's Studio, Nambucca Heads.

Tomorrow we are all going up to see Perth. I had better see all I can now, for goodness knows when we will return. We seem to do nothing but eat here, really. I get sick of the sight of food. I'm keeping a diary so that I can tell you all of my experiences when I come back. Some of the nurses are so pretty. Lovely colours. We had church again this morning. All the crew, doctors and sisters.

Miss Irene Brown the actress is on board, also Dr. Hoare from Mackay. He is always very nice, and has a yarn to me often. All our letters are read before posting, we are not allowed to say numbers or mention anybody. We got a wireless through last night to say that Italy had declared war, but it is not reliable. It won't be long now if it is true, I don't think I shall stay a day longer after the war. I feel Queensland-sick now.

We are calling at Bombay after Colombo, then Aden and Port Said. I am looking forward to see Bombay. Hope Bob is keeping better, poor old fellow. *(One of her younger brothers, later died in his twenties from Bright's Disease).* Give them a kiss for me, I have only sent p.c. to my friends. I can't settle down to write, so send my letters to Doll and Andy.

Heaps of love, dear ones, to you all from

Queenie.

Postcard from Perth,
24th May, 1915.

Dearest Mum,

Just a p.c. from Perth post office, have written you a letter also. Hope you are all well. Having a grand time. Heaps of love,

Queenie

Chapter 3: Farewell Australia

S.S. Mooltan,
27th May, 1915.

Dearest Mother and boys,

We have been at sea now since Monday. Hope you get all the cards I send you. The weather is simply beautiful. We had a dance last night. I had every one and all the dances are so different, even a waltz is just like dipping and stepping all after rag-time. I even ragged, never did it in my life before either.

I realized my leave-taking, more than anytime, at Fremantle. Had a long look at dear old Australia. Our letters are to be strictly censored. We are not to give any information in numbers or names of ports, so it will be very hard to write letters. However, you know our next port of call, and we are all looking forward to seeing it and having a rickshaw ride. All going up to the Galle Face Hotel from the ball.

You will think we are all thinking of pleasure, but it is so funny being at sea and not hearing any war news. Our wireless is dismantled at Fremantle even, however it was posted up as a certainty about Italy just before we sailed so surely when we reach our next port we will hear some good news. I hope the war won't last much longer although it really hasn't started. The Germans are not out of France yet.

This is Andy's birthday. I wish he could have come along in the Red Cross as an orderly. It would have been splendid for him.

29th May, 1915.

All our letters are to be in with the censor before tomorrow so I must finish this today. Yesterday the weather was very squally and a monsoon started before the evening. The whole top deck was wet. The evening before we went to the Second Class saloon for a concert given by the New South Wales troops. It was very good, some of them are great musicians.

Every day we have a lecture and drill, we have been vaccinated, but it is so hard to tell you news as the censors are so strict. I can't even tell you our orders. Lieutenant Colonel Stawell from Melbourne gave us a lecture one afternoon on the work of Florence Nightingale. It was very interesting.

It's great fun at night after dinner getting on to the top deck for the best corners. One beating the other. It is fearfully hot and we shall be passing the Equator tomorrow morning. There are not to be any jokes. Too many on board. I often wonder what you are all doing. When I come back it will take days to tell you all the doings I shall hate to leave the "Mooltan" at Egypt.

I have a great chum, Nurse Donnelly, she is Jean Casey's cousin, very much like her – in some ways, but not a bit with character, she is very firm and determined. She is going to England though so we part later on. Everybody is writing letters, the decks are crowded, most of the nurses brought their own chairs but I did not get one. However, I always have one to sit on. Fancy you can't get one from the boat. I am still keeping a diary so you can read it.

The "Mooltan" is not so big as I expected it to be. We have a sports club on board and several games are on. There is also a paper to be issued which will be very interesting and funny, I'm sure. Hope I shall hear from you all the week after I arrive, there is a mail boat every fortnight and sometimes every week. Heaps of love and kisses to you all,

Queenie xxxxxxxxx

Letter to Queenie's older brother, Andrew Richard Avenell, who lived to the age of eighty-eight years.

S.S. Mooltan
30th May, 1915

Dear Andy,

I have only written to Mother so far, but she is sending my letters on to you. Miss Irene Brown, the actress, is playing the piano while I am writing. She can play too, but I don't like her at all. She is so conceited and ugly. We are all having a glorious time.

I cannot tell you any of our movements as our letters are strictly censored. I am keeping a diary, though, so you can see it on my return. There is a crowd on board and we have a sports club, games and dances. It is an experience for me and I thank God I became a nurse, otherwise I should never have got this chance. Our next port of call will be very interesting, you must know where it is by the date, we are going for rickshaw rides etc. War was declared in Italy the day we left Fremantle so there will be something doing by the time we reach our destination, eh!

I had a great old time in Melbourne and Adelaide and Perth. Dr. Hoare is on board, I am allowed to mention that as he is not a soldier. He looks terribly worn and thin and needs a good rest, but he is the same as ever. I saw "High Jinks" in Melbourne. It was grand. "This is the Life" is awfully catchy, everybody is singing it. We have lectures and drill every day. Shall write again. Heaps of Love from

Queenie xxxxxx

P.S. I thought of your birthday. Hope your back well again soon. I wish you were with us in the Red Cross, they are such a splendid lot of fellows. Q

Letter posted 2nd June, 1915, after Colombo, on Galle Face Hotel stationery.

Dearest Mother and all at home,

We had lunch at this place, it is a very gay and oriental hotel. Bazaars all round. We arrived Colombo 4 a.m. got up at 5 a.m. in our kims *(kimonos)* to see the harbour. Oh dear, I did love our day. We had breakfast at the Grand Oriental Hotel, and motored from 9.30 till 1 p.m.

Major L. Gibson and Major McLean took Sister Donnelly and me. No one was allowed off the boat unprotected. We went out to Mt. Lavinia through all the native streets. Saw their museum which was awfully interesting. We seemed to pass hundreds of various bungalows. Really, I don't know where we didn't go. Our escorts were more than kind to us. Major McLean bought me a silver necklet and an ivory elephant, also a book of one hundred views of Ceylon.

Most of the things were very dear, or at least they asked us big prices, and then if we didn't buy they would run after us and say, take it at half price. We rickshawed along the beach. Sister used to have a dozen or more of the fellows running after her begging. We laughed and laughed. Silk was very dear. There was a riot in amongst the natives; they were killing each other, the Cingalese and Mohammedans.

I feel a bit tired of the boat. It is three weeks tomorrow since we left Sydney, and we have another ten days to go before we reach Port Said. We reach Bombay tomorrow, and supposed to stay two days. It is unusual to call there so we are lucky to see it. I find it hard to keep clean, think I will have to get some blouses tomorrow. We can't wear our uniforms, it is so dreadfully hot. We all sleep upstairs, too hot down in the cabins. It won't be so bad though after leaving Bombay. The Red Sea is worse though, of course. We left Colombo at eight o'clock at night, never stayed the night after all, but we had a long day and felt very tired when we got back to the boat.

We hear all sorts of rumours, about the canal. Some say it is not safe and we are to be kept at Port Said and of course it's made worse than it really is. Seventy-five passengers got on at Colombo, so the boat is packed. We had a parade in honour of the King's birthday yesterday and sang "God Save The King". I haven't written any letters at all, but I can't say anything, so they would be uninteresting. This is being posted with one of the officer's mail, so it can be censored ashore.

I should love to spend a holiday in Colombo. It is so quaint, but it is terribly hot. The Grand Oriental Hotel is very nice, but the Galle Face is better situated, and I would love to stay a few weeks there. I suppose you remember it all coming out. We had a great visit all day and I did love it. We hear very little war news. It seems to be very isolated from the world and we are far ahead in lots of ways.

Hope you are all keeping well. I feel very homesick today. We may not be allowed to get off at Bombay as there is a plague outbreak, but I believe there is always plague there. Heaps of love to you all, send this on to Doll and Andy, Mum

xxxxxxxxxx Hope Bobo is better

Q xxxxxxxxx

Taj Mahal Palace Hotel, Bombay,
10th June, 1915.

Dearest Mother and boys,

I am writing you these few lines just before we reach our next port. We had a glorious time in Bombay and like it very much. Going round all the bazaars and markets, I did not buy much, as I hadn't the money to spare, but saw some lovely Indian scarfs, etc. I sent several P.C.s last mail to you; all our letters are strictly censored.

The sea is like a mill-pond and so blue. Really, the weather has been splendid, but for the heat, but then, that is the usual thing, we have not struck one decent monsoon so far. There are hundreds of little flying fish – shoals of porpoises jumping up and racing us. The trip seems very long and I shall really be glad to get to Cairo. It sounds funny but we are all alike, you get very tired of seeing the same people every day. We just saw two immense whales and two boats passed today. I spent the afternoon on the poop deck watching the "Gyptian Sports". They were very good. Tug-O-War, Siamese Race, obstacle race, and all sorts of sports.

I have eleven boys to lecture to every day – eight of them are students from Melbourne University and in their first year of medicine. One of them is a master of science, but all I have to tell them is on nursing; they will be our orderlies, you know. We have dances every other night. Auction bridge and deck quoits. I won my heat yesterday. I can't get over the calmness of the sea. It is just like the Brisbane River.

Dr. Hoare is looking much better than when he came on, and he looks after me very well too. I can mention his name as he is not a military man, you see. I do wish you were here. I have such lots to tell you, but never mind, wait till I come home. Hope you are all well, and Bob is not taking any more bad turns. I always think of you when I see anything fresh.

Heaps of love

xxxxxxx Queenie

Chapter 4: Egypt

Postcard from Port Taurig,
15th June, 1915.

To Mrs R. G. Avenell, Townsville:

Hope you are all well. Takes six hours get to Cairo and then thirty minutes to Heliopolis. Love Q.

P.S. We have not had any money given to us yet, but I still have some left, so don't worry.

Sultan Ibrahim Palace, Heliopolis,
22nd June, 1915.

Dearest Mum and all at home,

I intended to write to you yesterday as it was my day off, but the previous night I got a wire from Uncle Harry *(Colonel Harry Lee, injured at Gallipoli on the day of the landing)* to meet him at the Cairo Railway station, so off I went. Just missed the train so yesterday Captain Fraser, an R.A.N.C. Doctor, took me out to see the sights of Cairo and look up Uncle. However, we did not see him, and when I got back, I found he had come out to Luna Park to see me, but was coming today which he did. He has altered very much, of course, to what I remember, and looks very careworn and old *(he was fifty-two years old).* Although very well and healthy, still one can tell he is just from the trenches. He injured his ankle and broke a small bone and has been in hospital at Alexandria.

One of our nurses off the Mooltan that went to Alexandria told him I was here, so he came down for a few days to see me. He is staying out at Gezirah at Mr Wells', the Minister for Education – some swanky people of Cairo, I might tell you. I had a great old yarn, and I collected all the 9th Battalion boys up before him and he sat down among them and yarned away while I went on doing my dressings. You know, I have thirty-six men to look after and there are dozens of dressings to be done. Really, our feet are simply dreadful by the end of the day. We all rub methylated spirit on them. One of my patients is a chap named Warburton from Townsville.

I enjoyed myself immensely yesterday. Had lunch at the Grand Continental and then we took a Gharry *(horse-drawn carriage)* all round the bazaars, visited some mosques and the Egyptian University, three thousand students, and the tombs of the Caliphs. We did not have to take our boots off but they put other shoes on our feet. The people were all praying and bowing low with their heads touching the floor and they wash themselves before leaving. The good Egyptian prays three times a day. It was all very interesting.

We also went through a shop of old brass and Persian rugs. They were very beautiful. We came back and had tea. Then went through the gardens and sat round the skating rink and watched the French girls skate. You know everything is French, shops and cafes, with the tables and chairs out on the streets. We had dinner out on the street at St. James Hotel. Band playing. The night does not begin until 10 p.m, dinner at 8.30 p.m. We then went to a music hall and stayed about an hour, then we motored home out to Heliopolis, which is about three miles away from Cairo. There are trams, Gharry and motors.

I am going to meet Uncle Harry tomorrow and go out to these friends for dinner. We were terribly busy today getting ready for new patients, which are expected to arrive tonight. There are numbers of wounded coming in (not allowed to state the exact number). The cases are most interesting where the bullets just missed important organs. The shrapnel are the deadly things. We took a shrap out of a man's throat today, he is one of the 9th, Isaacs from Townsville, too. It was as big as a marble.

Poor beggars, all the arms and legs with shrapnel wounds. It is a great strain, and it is a good thing we can get a half day every other day, off-duty. I can't write any letters to my friends, I am on the go all the time, and my feet are too sore. I am nearly dropping off to sleep now. There are two other nurses in my room they are groaning and moaning.

You know, this is a beautiful building, a real harem too. I wish a sultan would come along, though Lieutenant Stoddart and Captain Mills took us out to dinner the other night to an Egyptian restaurant. It was very funny – every meal you have rock and water melon. There are lovely grapes just now, but I can't eat the butter. Yes, it's cruel!

We heard today they are going to take the big hill tomorrow over at the Dardanelles. It is Kitchener's birthday and they intend to celebrate it by having a great go at the Turks. One of the boys told me bullets used to fly round them and they would get off scot-free.

Well dearie and all, I am dog-tired so goodnight, tons of love.

xxxxxxx Queenie.

Gordon House, Heliopolis,
29th June, 1915.

Dearest Mother and all at home,

Although I am dog-tired I am going to write you a few lines on your birthday and wish you many happier years to come. I had my fortune told me at Colombo and then here out at the Pyramids the other day and they both were the same. My life is to be much better and brighter from now on. I am to be very rich, also a lot of other rot. However I hope some of it is true for your sake.

Well, I would give anything to be back in Australia just now. Really, the heat is awful and the work fearfully strenuous. I still have my ward on Section in the Pavilion. A rumour went round today that we are going up to Alexandria, but it may only be a yarn. Uncle Harry *(Colonel Harry Lee, Commander of the 9th Battalion, said to be the second person to land at Gallipoli, who was wounded same day)*, left on Saturday. I don't suppose he will come back. A lot of our men shall be "finished" (as the Arabs say here), before they get the hill.

We don't hear any news here at all, except from the boys themselves and they can only tell you little of where they are. They don't even get much news. I have met several old patients some are going home with bad legs and arms. There are some marvellous escapes, really. Bullets and shrapnel flying through them just above their hearts. One man in my ward had a bullet go through his mouth out of his neck and again in and out of his shoulder. He is going back to the Dardanelles later.

I am collecting some great snaps. Those I sent you last week are real photos of the Gallipoli Peninsula taken on the spot. The boys told me there were cameras and glasses all along the beach. They had to throw them down.

Major McLean took Sister Tyson and me out to the Pyramids. They are much bigger than I expected and the drive out is glorious, beautifully made roads all round and we went down into King Pharoah's and his daughter's tomb by the Sphinx. We had our photos taken on the camels. You know, you get out of the motor about three hundred yards away from the pyramids and ride camels, they are lovely creatures. I was a bit scared.

Those little Arabs holding the water jugs, scream out immediately the photo is taken for "baksheesh", meaning "present" or "money", everything is money or piastres. The boys call them "disasters". We had dinner at the Continental after our outing and the band played some beautiful things. The dinner tables are right out in the open on the street, with all pretty shaded lamp shades. They eat and smoke away. I had some Egyptian cigarettes – six Egyptian cigarettes. All women smoke.

I had dinner with Uncle at Gezireh. He stayed with the Director of Education, a big stone house, and very nice people. I don't care much for Uncle though, he is all for show. I kept him waiting an hour for me, couldn't help it. He is looking very worn and old. Of course, he has been through a great strain. You can tell. I hope for Auntie's sake he will get on. He came down from Alexandria just to see me. There are some lovely buildings at Heliopolis and Cairo. Plenty of Turks here too. I am now living at Gordon House. Was very glad to get away from the harem. Went out to afternoon tea at the camp one day. Poor beggars, the sand is dreadful. Well Mum, any time I may be moved, they want nurses for transport work. I don't want to go. Hope you are all well.

Heaps of love and kisses from,

Queenie

Sister Theresa Tyson, Major Hector McLean and Queenie at the Pyramids, 1915.

Gordon House, Heliopolis,
6th July, 1915.

Dearest Mother and all at home,

It is my afternoon off, so I must drop you my weekly letter. I am now nursing at the Palace, but only relieving, while the nurses who came over in January are having a week up at Alexandria. I am then supposed to be going to the Golf Club, which is being opened up as a hospital. We heard unofficially the boys had taken the hill, but one can't believe a thing over here. There are such a lot of yarns going around.

We all go to the Heliopolis Hotel, out on the piazza in the evening either before we go into Cairo or when we come home. It is the rendezvous for the military officers, of course. We are officers and you sit out in the open, band, and pictures, all the time ices and drinks on the go. We meet crowds of people we know. It is a very gay place now in the summer, so what will it be like in the winter?

I got my first pay, four pounds, the other night. It should have been eight so I was glad to find out if you were getting yours. I don't want any more money, for we are taken everywhere and only need a few piastres or "disasters", the boys call them. I was nursing, (two hundred in the ward), Typhoid, Pneumonia and Dysentery, all back from the Dardanelles.

I got a letter from Auntie Palmer *(Aunt Emily Palmer, previously Emily Avenell, widowed 1901 and re-married in 1903 and living in Ilford, London)* so am sending it on to you. I hope I shall be picked for transport duty to England. Twelve nurses left for the Dardanelles. Had a letter from Dr. Ross, he is in Surrey and coming out to the Dardanelles also. I cannot find out where Norman Mighell is, they tell me he is wounded in the jaw, but don't know where he is. I suppose he has gone to Malta. His mother gave me a parcel for him.

Such a lot of the boys are suffering from shock and nervous breakdown. I often wonder how you all are; every nurse got letters but me. The first mail since we landed. I was very disappointed. I think when the war is over we won't be able to get back to Australia quick enough, really. Every nurse feels the same. Cairo is very interesting. I would never get tired of looking and seeing all there is, but dear old Australia for me every time.

There are three places where the officers go at night and meet French, Greek, Italian, and all races of beautiful women. They drink and dance with them and then if they wish can go back to their flats with them. Of course, the managers of these places employ the girls and won't let them go away until 10.30 p.m. then they can do as they like. No ladies ever go near these places, but I believe all the men go there. One place is called the "Casino". No Privates are allowed. It is a hot place, alright.

The sisters are treated very well, all due respect etc, and we do have a good time off duty, work hard all day too. I went out to the Zoo last week it was very interesting, we are going to the Kersaal tonight, a music hall variety show, etc. Decent place. I was with Nurse Gibbon's little sister today. She came over with Echlin. I don't see much of them, we live in different places and have different time off.

The buildings are very massive and all stone here. Very dirty and dusty walking anywhere, but a Gharry takes us everywhere for a few piastres, such nice comfortable carriages they are. Good horses too. When we go out in a car, we all get in, look comfortable as though staying for a week, they *(local drivers)* say "How much to Cairo?" Whatever he says you offer half the amount, and if he doesn't agree, (have never heard one satisfied straight away yet), you all get up and out and walk away. Then they come chasing us calling out your fare. We always have to beat them down, I get sick of them, and glad to get away from them.

(Page missing, as there is no signature)

No. 1 General Hospital, Heliopolis,
11th July, 1915.

Dear Mother and boys,

Got your short letter yesterday dated the 27th May, the only letter I have received since I left Australia. I heard also yesterday that conscription is in Australia, so both Andy and Jim will be over here and very few of them will return. The hill is not taken yet. In three weeks they are supposed to be in Constantinople.

Captain Birkbeck came in again a few nights ago, (a bullet wound just above the eye) injured, nothing really so he must be a lucky man, his third wound. He is going back for the third time next week. I am at the Palace now in the medical ward nursing Dysentery, Typhoid, Rheumatism and Pneumonia, from the trenches mostly, and of course, some are only from the camp. We have thirty cases in the Hall "Magnificent" room, brass fittings round the chandeliers and walls. The room is very elaborately fitted too. Then we go down some marble steps into the rotunda, and from that out on to the piazza.

The place is beautiful alright, but we haven't any time to admire the rooms, and it makes you terribly tired just walking round half one storey. I was going out to Helouan, *('Al Hayat', the Australian Convalescent Home),* 20 miles away, this afternoon per motor with one of the officers, but he was sent off for a few hours this morning very cool and nice, but I mustn't growl as it is war and have to get used to disappointments. Yesterday we arranged to go to the Citadel, but could not go so I'm not going to make any more appointments.

Some of the nurses who came over in January are looking very run down. Twenty of us are told to be packed ready to start at a minute's notice for somewhere, might be transport or anything. We are all going on transport duty to the Dardanelles, so that will be getting nearer. There is a base Hospital at Gallipoli. I am terribly tired at night but have a good rest always when I do get to bed. Have been out motoring every night this week and could go out with heaps of gentlemen. They just love to take us, and the fresh air does us good. I went three nights running to the Pyramids. They are better in the moonlight.

Got a letter from one of the nurses at Innisfail yesterday, and Ivy Auld from Mt. Perry is going there as Matron so I'm glad they have someone. Well, mother, this is a funny place it has one great thing we can't get away from and shall never forget either and that's Cairo's smell.

Well, we had an orchestra from 2 p.m. till 5 p.m. in the hall at the Palace, weird and charming. I felt I could cry out. Seeing all the boys round me and this beautiful music. I often think I should not go out and enjoy myself, but it wouldn't do me any good to stay at home. Some of the patients get terribly affected with it and think they are fighting again. They are all more or less suffering from the severe strain and shock. The ear and eye ward is next to mine and would make you sick to see the blind young men about twenty and their hair almost white. Shells, explosives and gas, but I mustn't say much as all our letters are censored. I don't suppose you will read half of this as it is.

The mail for Australia closes tomorrow and I must finish this today. "The Mooltan" just came. Finish this tonight.

(Page 5 missing, Page 6 pinned to letter dated 11th July, 1915, first words missing.)

... come to Sydney or Melbourne to meet me. I drew my pay today, once a fortnight I get ten shillings a week clear and then every month I get our field allowance of one and nine pence a day. Tell Bob and Len and Jim to write to me. Poor old Doll, I s'pose is getting nearer her time.

Heaps of love to you all and kisses

xxxxxxxx Queenie

No. 1 Australian General Hospital, Heliopolifs,
24th July, 1915.

Dear Mother and all at Home,

My room mate and I have both got the blues, so I am going to try and shake mine off and write some letters. The damn flies are so bad, they creep and crawl all over one and are quite tame. They swarm round the natives' eyes. Rotten things, sometimes we have a man to switch them when doing dressings.

I think I wrote and told you I was back from the Palace. Relieved a fortnight, and had three deaths. So feel glad to get away. Our place is for convalescence, so we never see many very sick cases, medical, I mean. They are run down and anaemic and have bad limbs, of course. I am sending you a photo of some of my patients. They are all going back to Australia and would have us taken.

We don't hear much news from the Dardanelles lately. No wounded have come down for some time. The No. 3 General Hospital have been sent back from England to Lemnos Island so they will be nearer than we are. Uncle Harry was in charge of that island for a while. I wonder how he is. Have not heard of him at all. I have not had any letters from anyone, so think they have gone astray. They travel round Cairo a few weeks sometimes.

We are going to the Citadel tonight. It is to be lit up with two thousand lights from 7.30 till 9.30. They have all Imperial patients. There also English doctors and nurses. Claude Lloyd came to see me last week; he is a corporal and a nice boy. Some people of Cairo gave the boys a grand concert last night. It was very nice. Lieutenant Kensett of 24th Battalion took me out to Helouan last Thursday afternoon, twenty miles down the Nile. We motored alongside the whole way, it was so pretty and I saw a lot of the boys from the Park.

They go out there when their wounds are healed and they are waiting to go home on leave. It is cooler than Cairo too, and they have a great time. I am going on a house boat to Barrage, another pretty place I believe, next Monday. I hope another sister and I are going to Oroski next Wednesday to get a few curios for you. I can't afford much but there are some funny things. Hope dear old Bob is keeping well and all of you too. Wish this war would end soon.

Heaps of love and kisses from

Queenie.

No. 1 Australian General Hospital, Heliopolis,
3rd August, 1915.

Dearest Mother,

We are still in the same place after being ready to move at a minute's notice. They have kept us here. I shall never forget "Luna Park" all the boys and their different wounds. Surely it can't go on much longer. We have not had many wounded in for some time, but a lot of medical cases from the trenches. It is three months now since they landed, and some came in yesterday from the first lot that landed, worn out, thin nervous, poor boys. The Turks will take some beating alright. Our men are waiting for the Tommies to take their position and then the Australians will close in.

I had a letter from Auntie Trot. She has just got your letter and said she wished she could have seen you. The weather is fearfully hot and such hot winds too. Shall be glad when it is all over. I am in my nightie lying down. My afternoon off, no-one ever goes out till 5 p.m. The flies make it almost impossible to write. You will think I am all growls, but really Mother, it is a pretty rotten place to live in, dry and dusty the whole time, rains one inch a year.

It is the wickedest place in the world; fancy, twenty-five thousand bad women in Cairo, all registered, and our troops had a riot this week. Burnt down some buildings in the low quarters. For some reason one of the soldiers was tackled while there, so the crowd got into the place. They are not allowed into Cairo now. They had to call out pickets and order all the boys home.

I have a man named Warburton now from Townsville leaving for Australia soon, really any day. He has had a shocking leg and was in Uncle's Battalion. So he will be able to tell you all about me. I shall give him your address and he can go and see you when he arrives. Have had two postcards from you now and a letter from Nurse Davis telling me all the news; she says they are getting new quarters and I won't know the place. Now, Mum I hope you are getting on alright and money matters are not worrying you too much. Write to me.

Heaps of love to you all.

From Queenie.

No. 1 Australian General Hospital, Heliopolis,
12th August, 1915.

My Darling Mum,

I am dead tired so cannot write many lines. We are having a rough and jolly busy time receiving patients galore. Our poor old boys they do look awful, such food and dirty, poor beggars. I got Dr. Taylor's son Waldon in my ward today, heaps of other nice boys too, and they have dysentery, influenza, etc. They have surrounded the hill at last, but it's not quite taken, our boys got it and two regiments of the British Army got blown up in the middle. I got a letter last night from Charlie Palmer and will enclose it. Fancy, he is over there and I may nurse him if he gets wounded. I hope he doesn't. Well, no letters from Australia for an age. I got eleven last time but that's a long while ago. I know such lots of letters go astray. I have written to you every week and sent P.C.s too, as well.

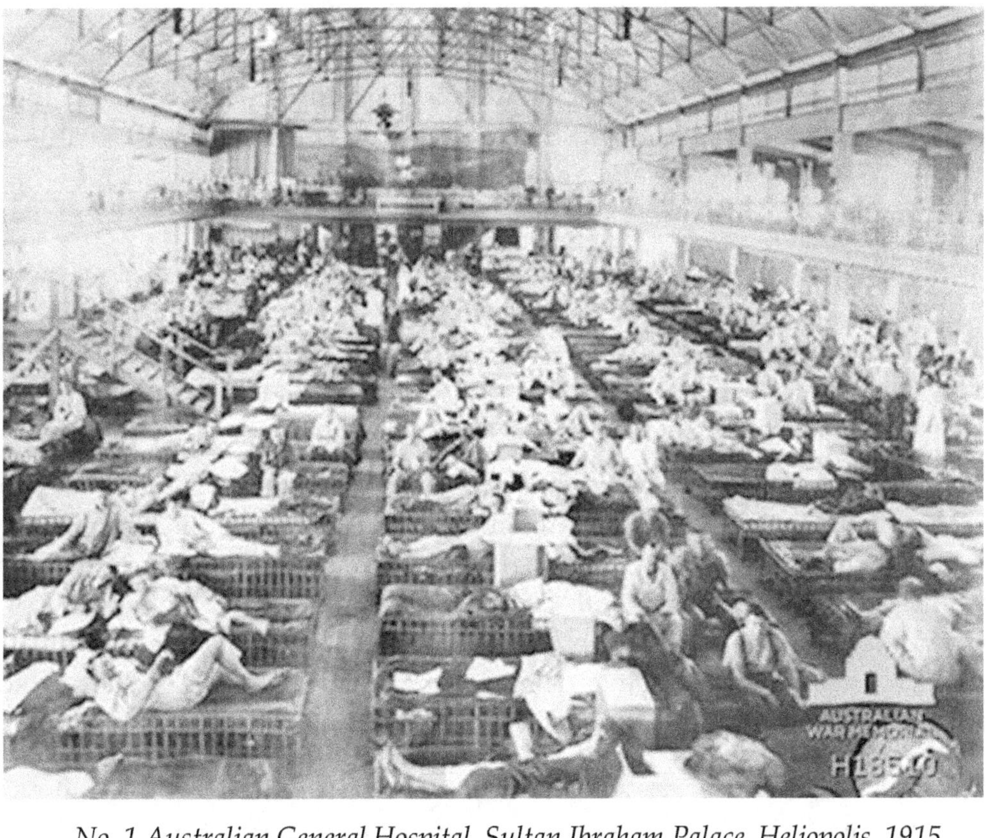

No. 1 Australian General Hospital, Sultan Ibraham Palace, Heliopolis, 1915.

Main ward containing wounded from Gallipoli. (AWM H18510)

Uncle Harry has gone back to Australia, a nervous breakdown they say. I have not heard of him at all. Colonel Stoddart is back in Alexandria with a nervous breakdown. This is the second attempt to write to you, Mum dear. We are now getting the actual war nursing. They come in all of a sudden and we just tear round and do dressings all day. They are doing well over at Achi Baba alright, but of course you know more about "971 Hill" and Achi Baba than we do, and I expect before this reaches you, the Dardanelles will be ours. I am dead tired, worked for 13 hours yesterday without a rest, eat my dinner, and off again.

Young Boddington from Mackay is in with us. He has his face knocked about with a shell explosion, a lucky escape. Some haven't any nose and look awful. Uncle Harry looked terribly nervy when I saw him. I got his batman in my ward a few days ago. He said he had left Gallipoli and was going back to Australia, so it must be true. This batman has given me a lot of souvenirs from over there. A Turkish Shell, which had been full of shrapnel. They have a brass screw top, all turkish writing, and measuring round it. They are very plentiful over there.

One Turkish gun the boys call it "Beachy Bill". Since the day they landed it has sent shells every day on to a part of the beach, so many a day, fancy, from a hill. I am afraid to say much as it is all censored, but the different yarns the boys tell us really it's awful. However the British army has suffered with this last charge, and the Australians came in at the end. Some say the 15th Battalion and 2nd Light Horse Queensland is almost wiped out. Two Brigades are leaving this week for Gaba Tepe so we won't have such a good time off-duty. It's just as well, for we are too busy and tired to go out now. It is still terrifically hot.

I was transferred to another hospital just opened up, "Abassia", and out on the desert, no good to me, so I asked to stay in "Luna Park" and am still here. No one can be spared for transport duty, so we don't expect to go yet. One of our nurses left for Australia with a boat of returning wounded yesterday. We heard we would only be here another three months. It will all be over then. I hope it is true.

Echlin and I went out for dinner with some officers going off this week. I am too tired to write anymore. Hope you are all right. I have enough money, although really we are paid badly, we have been given an extra mess allowance. Before, we had to pay our mess account with some piastres of our salary, which meant I hardly got one pound per fortnight, however it is better now. You are not getting very much from me, but I hope to do something more when I come back, which might be in six months some say.

Shall write again next week. Lots of love to you all

xxxx Queenie.

No. 1 Australian General Hospital, Heliopolis,
22nd August, 1915.

Dearest Mum and boys,

I have sent you all some posties, but as the mail closes tomorrow, thought you would like a letter too. Although I am so tired. I think that's what we all seem to be saying all over the place. We have one long day then the next afternoon off-duty, but our long day is very strenuous. Start dressing the wounds at 8.30 a.m. and go until 7.40 p.m. at night. Of course, some vary, some may only need the one dressing, and others might be four-hourly.

We are getting over the rush now, since the charge at Gaba Tepe. Wasn't it awful about the boat going down? Some of the patients coming from Gallipoli said they passed two miles of wreckage floating with the current. Boats overturned, soldier's helmets, caps, kits, and the inside of the ship, oh dear, it's too wicked. We were so relieved to hear it wasn't our boys.

Haven't had a letter from Dolly since I left. Glad to hear she is keeping well and Len and Bob had a good time with her at Ayr. A young fellow named Summerville is in my section from Ayr. He told me he was in love with Nurse Gifford. Waldron Taylor is almost better. Had a letter from Coley last mail.

I have such a fine shrapnel explosive to bring back as a souvenir. Of course, it is Turkish. Also, have a clip of Turkish bullets, a large Turkish button with the crescent and star. Uncle Harry's batman gave me all these things. He has gone back to the front again. Uncle, I told you, is at Malta with dysentery.

Well, I must tumble into bed. Heaps of love to you all. Sorry to hear you have to shift again, but twenty-seven shillings and sixpence is a bit too much for that place, isn't it? Shall not be away much longer now.

Queenie.

Staff at No.1 Australian General Hospital, Heliopolis, 1915. Sister Queenie Avenell is pictured at the front far right. (AWM P00173.001)

No. 1 Australian General Hospital, Heliopolis,
24th August, 1915.

Dear Mother and boys,

I am on night duty now for a month and somehow tonight I felt so near you all. So I am just going to write to you a few lines. It is not nearly so strenuous at night, but still it's bad enough. We are getting over our last rush, but expect trains in any time tonight.

I wrote you a letter about four days ago and sent you some snaps. They are not good of me, and I don't look as miserable as they look. I have got a bit thinner though. Am only just getting my feet and legs used to the tiled floors, oh dear, they did ache at night, but I was a bit collar proud you know.

We do love our patients, they are such bricks with their awful wounds. One of my patients was hit with shrapnel in five different places, his eye blown out. Left arm blown off and other wounds on the back and body. He is a brave fellow. He says he is not too bad, but he thinks he got more than his share. Waldron Taylor is better and going out to Helouan tomorrow. Helouan is a convalescent place. The Palace takes all bed cases and clear their beds to ours, sometimes there is an overflow, we send them on to Helouan or Teiloun. From there they either go back to their unit or Australia.

I have not seen any Queensland papers since I arrived. Nor a casualty list for ages. Our O.C. Colonel M. Smith is going back to Australia. We find it very hot to sleep in the day, but I sleep from 10 – 4 p.m. Today I felt quite fit to go on duty alright. I am going out with Echlin and Gibbon tomorrow to do some shopping. It is all white over here. We can't wear anything else, too hot. The nights are very cold.

We climbed up the water chute tonight and had a view of the country. The 1st Light Horse are camped alongside us, and we could see rows of tents all round. We are very military, reveille is always going and bugle calls. I had a motor run all round the native quarters one afternoon last week. It was so funny and different to Australia. The natives are always yelling out "Baksheesh" meaning money or present. They touch you if you let them. We just say "Emshee". We can speak quite a number of dialect words.

Well, Mum, foment calls me.

Heaps of love to you all, from

Queenie.

1st Australian General Hospital, Heliopolis,
28th August 1915.

Dearest Mother and Boys and Doll,

I wrote you a letter some days ago, but I was so tired and sleepy I forgot whether I put it in the right envelope. There was nothing in it that I would be afraid for anyone to see, so if it turns up in a strange way you will understand I am on night duty. Think I told you, have two hundred and fifty patients, mostly convalescents, young Fox from "Bombardie" is one of them. He says poor Edward Williams from "Burrenbring" was killed right beside him, you know he is from Mackay. Everybody seems to be having sorrow and losses in their family now. Poor bright Lucy Wright I saw, died of pneumonia in Melbourne too. I motored out to Helouan yesterday afternoon. It is such a pretty run all along the Nile and the roads are just perfect with trees on either side.

(Top of Page 2 torn.)

I am quite getting used to soldiers now. Bugles all day and reveilles, and every morning the horses go by, miles of them being exercised, one man has four, rides one and holds three. It is the Light Horse. The men are over at the peninsula. They were so disappointed not being able to take their horses with them. The Sixth Brigade is leaving tomorrow for Anzac, so they will be marching past. As soon as we hear the band, we all fly to look out at them. They often pass on a route march playing the band. I have not had any letters for weeks now, in fact no one has, so the mail must be late. I have a night off next Friday, so Sister Hodgson and I are going up to Alexandria for the day just to have a swim. They have a lovely beach I believe. Have written Will Lee to meet us...

(Top of Page 3 missing)

(Regarding the heat) ... there won't be much left of us after the war is over, brown grease spots. We have all decided to secure a husband while we are over here, as the boys will be so few and such heroes, the girls in Australia will rush them, and no one will bother about us. I have had several proposals, but none I like, "my fis" with them, that's Arabic for "the end". "Baksheesh" means money or present. I can't write the dozens of words I know. Can talk them though, the

natives, Arabs and poor dirty Egyptians, cry out to us "baksheesh" and we say "Emshee Yalla" or it sounds like that; it means "Clear Out". "Eshma" means "Come Here" and "stanna", "stop". "Messquish" means "no good".

(Top of Page 4 missing)

The Egyptian men ... with their little scarlet Fez on... are mad for women and keep heaps of wives. I have not been inside a harem, but am going to, before I come away. The women are so pretty and wear flowing coloured silk gowns and sit on beautiful rugs and cushions. Well, Mum, I must end off. My patients all have the nightmare – killing Turks, and yelling out. They always do a week after they come from Gallipoli. Quieten down later on. It is so severe on their nerves. Poor chaps. I do think it is a shame they have to go and put up with all this for the sake of the war. I have made such a lot of friends, but they might be taken.

Heaps of love to you all, Doll and Ken and babies.

Queenie xxxxxxxx

Front of a dugout at Gallipoli, with members of the 10th Light Horse pictured. From Queenie's photo album.

No. 1 Australian General Hospital, Heliopolis,
6th September, 1915.

Dear Mother and boys,

Just got your letters. Glad to hear you are all well and fancy having to move again. What a nuisance! I liked that place so much too. Well, we are still busy. I come off night-duty in a fortnight, thank goodness. Although someone must do it, and it's over now. I slept from 9.30 a.m. till 4 p.m. today so that is not too bad.

I got up and went out by 5 p.m. An officer called with a motor for me and we whizzed into town for tea at Shepheard's Hotel. A string band playing the whole time. Echlin was on the piazza too, so we had a merry time. We then motored round Gezireh and home in time for duty at 7.40 p.m. back to my soldier boys. They are such hard cases and do tease me. They were all imitating animals tonight, cats, fowls, calfs, etc. I said I thought I was nursing heroes not animals of the Zoo, which made them worse, of course.

I had a night off so Sister Hodgson (Matron, Kilcoy) and myself went up to Alexandria for the day. We get free passes. It was great we went into the briny (Mediterranean Sea) for a swim. We missed Billie Lee, though. He met the wrong train, and then did not know where we were staying, so we had no time to look him up. We met two officers we knew and they came with us. I never saw Bill after all. *(Queenie's cousin, Captain 'Billie' H.W. Lee, 9th Battalion).*

Alexandria seems much cleaner than Cairo, not nearly so interesting, but the sea makes such a difference, you know how we love the sea. The hotel we stayed at "The Majestic" was very eastern; we had a room on the top floor away up in the clouds. Our doors opened out on to little balconies. It cost us fifteen shillings for the trip altogether, and of course, we got a pass on the train. The fare is two pounds return otherwise. We had no time to go to any hospitals. It was a bit of a rush. I shall send you some snaps we took.

I like Sister Hodgson very much. We seem to be receiving more medical cases from the peninsula lately. Am very tired and nodding so "Goodnight". Heaps of love to you all. Shall write soon as I will be off night-duty soon and won't have so much time.

xxxxx Queenie.

No. 1 Australian General Hospital, Heliopolis,

9th September, 1915.

Dearest Mother and boys,

So glad to get your letters this week and to hear you are settled down again such a bother shifting about, I'm sure you must just loathe the thought of it now. I am enclosing three pounds with this, I don't want it. You know we are taken about everywhere in motors and I have plenty of clothes, so it might buy Len and Bob some clothes. It is my field allowance. I only wish I could let you have more every fortnight, however I can send you a little like this now and again.

I took young Freddie Fox (Bombardie) out to Cairo with me this afternoon. He said I am the first Australian girl he has spoken to for twelve months. He was in the trenches for four months and is not wounded, only run down and a bit feverish at first. We did some shopping and then he would come home in a motor, so we just flew along. The roads are so good for motoring we will all be very spoilt. He has money so don't mind him spending it. He was glad to meet someone he knew. Evelyn Lascelles is in England, *(closely related to the Royal Family, from North Queensland),* but I daresay he has gone either back to the front or Australia by now.

Have been on night duty three weeks tomorrow so only have another week. Thank goodness. Did I tell you I saw Nurse Derrer? She's over at the No. 2 Ghezireh *(Hospital)* and *(Nurse Ellen)* Chidgey arrived last week, so Mackay nurses are being well represented. I got a late pass last night and went out to Shepheard's Hotel for dinner with an officer, who left for Gallipoli today. We had a nice time, large bottle of fizzy, but when we were coming home he took off his belt and stars and asked me to mind them for him. I felt rotten for he may never come back, however I have known him since first I came here and he is very fond of me, but I am not in love with him. Don't believe I ever shall be with any man. Well, I have put them in the bottom of my box. They go off *(are killed),* just the same as a Private you know, no difference at all.

I think I have written to you since I took a flying trip up to Alexandria. Never saw Will Lee, we bungled up our meets and trains and even where we stayed, but he is coming down to Cairo. We had a dip in the briny.

Uncle, you know Mother, has never been in the trenches for months, he only stayed a few days after landing. I think myself he is not fit and won't ever be. He is not young. Willie Lee has never been on Gallipoli for more than a few hours. He has been stationed at Alexandria the whole time. Of course, that's not his fault. Someone has to stay to look after their things and he was made transport officer in Brisbane. But Auntie or Grandad need not worry about them. Major Robertson has been made Colonel, and Uncle, I believe, is going back to Australia as medically unfit.

They say the landing at Gallipoli is the grandest event in the world. Mons battle is not in it, so I suppose Uncle is suffering the effects, bombs, shrapnel and bullets whizzing everywhere. My word, those wounded soldiers that have gone back ought to be well treated. They had some terrible wounds. *(See editor's note below re Colonel Lee).* I am motoring out to the "Barrage" 30 miles away tomorrow (with a Private this time).

We have a topping time off-duty and night duty is so much quieter and restful. The ward just now is very amusing, admitted a number tonight and they all have the nightmare some were banging into the Turks yelling out and calling their mates. They are all like that at first the reaction of course. Achi Baba *(a hill overlooking Cape Helles on the Gallipoli Peninsula)* is still doing some dirty work with the Tommies *(English soldiers).*

How is poor old Doll? I always mean my letters for them all. I do wish Andy could get away to the war. He must feel it very much. Write again to me like you all did this week. Jim could write often too.

Heaps of love.

xxxxx Queenie

P.S. I shall not enclose money this letter, I have to get English notes.

Excerpt from a letter from Private Ray Baker, 9th Battalion, to his girlfriend Vera, describing the landing at Gallipoli. Private Baker was from Gympie, Queensland, where Queenie was born:

"Malta, May 1915.

…But the first day was the worst for us and we suffered rather severely.

Old Colonel Lee was heard to exclaim, 'Oh, my poor ninth, my poor ninth, they will be cut to pieces, they are bearing the brunt of it all.' I believe he was shot in the hand…. Most of the officers of the 9th were wounded, two or three, I believe, being killed… But we did our work and that was: to gain a footing on Gallipoli Peninsula and keep it…"

No. 1 Australian General Hospital, Heliopolis,
14th September, 1915.

Dearest Mum and boys,

Just a few lines to catch the mail which closes at midday. Well, everything seem at a standstill here lately. Yesterday and today all supposed to be a great charge at Gallipoli. So we will have another rush of wounded. Tomorrow they are taking a regiment of Light Horse over. The first horses sent over so far. I do hope they will all come to some decision soon and just come out on top.

Mum, I made such a nice friend, a Lieutenant C. Cunningham and he was so good and nice to me. He went to the front I got three letters from him, and this week his pal wrote to say he is killed. I feel I can't meet any more of them now. I had just written him a letter. His name is in the gazette today. He was a Ceylon tea planter and was attached to the Royal Minster Fusiliers 29th Division. He was such a fine fellow.

I feel very down in the dumps. We go out and have such gay times before they go off to the front and then we never see them again. It's wicked and I hate the very mention of war. Although we never get away from it, it is with us day and night. My latest news is that Sisters were asked yesterday to put their names down on a notice list for volunteers for a hospital in England. Hodgson and I have put ours down. If we are accepted we sail on the 20th of this month and I shall send you a weekend cable.

Oh, you have never mentioned if you received my cable I sent you when we arrived. It was more for your birthday. I sent it. It cost me five shillings. Perhaps you did not get it. Letters seem very easily lost over here. Another friend of mine went off last week. He gave me his belt and stars to keep on his return. I wonder if he will. It's really heartbreaking to see the boys and their wounds.

I am enclosing some snaps of some of the night nurses. We are a happy lot in a way. I had a letter from Auntie Trot tonight. Wouldn't she get a great surprise if I go home to England? It is to be a Commonwealth Hospital and nurse our own boys. We are not in love with the Tommies, you know. They have not got half the attraction or go, our boys have. We are to join the "Morea" at Port Said. I don't know if it is certain yet but however I shall certainly spend another five shillings and cable you.

I heard today our Queen Lizzie dreadnought was torpedoed some time ago, and the transport boats that went over a week ago, and Brigadier-General Legge was so long in the water he died of shock. Of course, this may be all lies. It is very dreadful if the "Old Lizzie", as the boys call her, has gone. She has done such a lot and they rely on her so much.

It is nearly five months since I left. I know you get heaps more news than we do. I love to get a Queenslander paper. Evelyn Lascelles is home in England. I had a game of tennis this afternoon. Another Sister and I went with two of our patients; they were so pleased to go out with an Australian. We motored thirty miles to the "Barrage". Had tea in some lovely gardens on the Nile and then got home in time for duty.

I am giving this letter to a patient in my ward. He is going home to Australia tomorrow. I started this letter last night but could not finish it as I knew the boys would take it if I missed the mail. I have some lovely views of Gallipoli trenches. Keep all the snaps I send you, Mum. I wonder how much longer I will be away. I shall try and get transport to Australia in three months.

Write to me soon, heaps of love to you all.

xxxxx Queenie.

No. 1 Australian General Hospital, Heliopolis,
21st September, 1915.

Dearest Mother,

I think this is my last night on night-duty. Matron has been up at Alexandria for a week and only returned yesterday, so I hope she will change us today. She has been over here ten months now and all the old nurses had a week's spell at Alexandria. I have been watching the troops go by the last hour, moving off to Gallipoli. They always pass "Luna Park", so we see them. They are a fine stamp of men and no mistake. The Territorials in Kitchener's army, as they call them, they're such weedy looking chaps. They are so merry looking and seem glad to be going over, knowing as they do what is before them. I think they are brave fellows. They are still passing by. The Army Service Corps now, I can hear the horses.

I admitted fifty-three new patients from the peninsula last night. All medical cases, in fact, there are very few wounded coming here now. They say everything is at a standstill. All they want is men. I believe forty thousand Italians and some Canadians are arriving on the peninsula, so we might hear of something doing shortly. Some say the war will last ten years and others give it eighteen months.

Well, I never went to England, I put my name down on the list which was fourteenth, and they only took six. I was just as well pleased at it is the cold winter just now and in about three months we can go, so I shall get in first next time. Hodgson went. I went in to see them all off (fifty altogether), some from every hospital. I have young Byers in from Hughenden, Hood from Brisbane, Gus McLean's brother of Magenta, Bogson from Cairns, and they appreciate my being a Queenslander. Eggflips are very acceptable after bully beef from the peninsula. They are fine fellows too.

We have to wear uniforms now always in and outdoor and helmets so it's just as well its getting cold. I don't look too bad, but "Oh dear", some of the old tarts? look breakups. I shall be glad to be back again in a short time from the end, or before, if they send me. We do get the blues at times, too much sadness and sickness around. I am dreaming of Turks all the time in my sleep. That's a sign of nerves alright. I dreamt of you yesterday though and thought I got home for a weekend and you cooked bacon and eggs for breakfast. So mind, that's my breakfast when I get home for sure. Well Mum about that money. I want it to be safe so I am arranging about a cheque for you with someone over here you see.

Heaps of love to you all,

Queenie

No. 1 Australian General Hospital, Heliopolis,
8th October 1915.

Dearest Mother,

I wrote you a hurried letter a few days ago. Everything I seem to do in Egypt is in a hurry. Am on the go day after day, and now when I'm off duty Rollie claims me, however he is going back to Gallipoli in a fortnight so I shall be less weary. This climate is awfully trying; it is quite hot again we had quite cold weather a week ago. I got Rollie to fix up a money order in Cairo. It can only be done in the morning and we only have a morning off once a fortnight, so I gave him the money and your address. He showed me the order and I saw it posted so I hope you get it safely. It will help pay that awful rent.

Well, it is rumoured on very good authority that we are all off to Italy shortly. If Rollie has to be sent back to Australia for wounds, or New Zealand. I shall get on a transport. We can go to the Dardanelles but I don't want to yet. It means once there on the hospital ship, never off it, so I shall just stay on here.

We motored out to Helouan yesterday afternoon and I took one of my patients with us and Grantie. It was lovely coming home. A long ride too all along the Nile and it is in flood just now. I shall never forget Egypt all my life. Although I am tired of it and would like to get away.

We have not heard definitely yet about the "Morea" but isn't it funny I was not taken at first? I was told to get ready, and then they did not take so many nurses, so I missed it. Poor old Hodgson was on board. I do hope they are all safe. Everyone is supposed to be saved and the boat beached, but no truth in yarns here. Shall have my photos next Wednesday so will send them on to you and Doll at once.

Poor old Doll, I know she would like one of her harem scarem Sister. I have made that four pounds on my mess allowance, so don't think I haven't much money, besides I am always taken everywhere and could go out three times as much if there were more than twenty-four hours in the day. I wonder was that wounded man in Townsville Warburton. He was one of the 9th.

Well, Mum I am going to get back to Australia after six months here. So shall fly* up to Townsville. Write to me every week.

Heaps of love to you all.

xxxx Queenie.

P.S. Rollie is such a man, Mother, and broadminded. I know you will like him. Q.

I wish this old war was over, we could get married and come back to see you together.

Editor's Note: Queenie's wartime fiancé, Rolland Arthur Reid, was tracked down from clues in her letters, as his last name is never mentioned. She says he was in Oliver "Trooper Bluegum" Hogue's unit and was mentioned twice in Oliver Hogue's famous World War I book, "Love Letters of an Anzac".

Rollie's older brother Lieutenant Lestock Henry Reid, born November 1885, Ardlin Rakaia, who is mentioned in Queenie's letter from Egypt 28th March, 1916, had just married his Irish cousin in England. He was killed in action on 20th May, 1916 and is buried in the Bonjean Military Cemetery, Armentiéres, France. He served with the New Zealand Pioneer Battalion at the first landing Gallipoli and was killed soon after arriving in France. (Information received from reference librarian, Rotearoa, New Zealand Library Christchurch, N.Z.)

Pat Richardson

**Figuratively speaking. Queenie would have taken the train from Brisbane to Gladstone, then ship Gladstone to Townsville to travel the one thousand, three hundred and eighty-four kilometres from Brisbane to Townsville.*

No. 1 Australian General Hospital, Heliopolis,
5th November, 1915.

Dearest Mother and family,

Well, I have just the same old news. I put my name down again for transport work. I would like to come back with the next lot of wounded. It takes exactly three months to go and come back. I get a fortnight's leave so could run up to you and have perhaps four days at home. I am calling up at the O.C.'s office today to try and manage it. I know there are heaps of others and their names are down. I would like to go to the Dardanelles very much.

Wasn't that a terrible thing about those poor New Zealand Nurses? They lowered a boat down on top of them and the poor girls had their limbs smashed and some were killed instantly. Of course, it could easily happen, they only had twelve minutes. And the ship disappeared and one sister was found singing "It's A Long Way To Tipperary" on a plank after being hours in the water. She was bucking the other boys up. Of course, Mother, we would not have that danger (on Transport) they were not on a hospital ship and volunteered to go. *(The sinking of the "Marquette", a British transport ship, near Salonika on October 23, 1915. Ten New Zealand nurses were drowned and all New Zealand Army hospital stores were lost, causing a great commotion in New Zealand, as hospital personnel and stores should not have been on this ship carrying munitions.)*

There are thousands of troops landing on the Canal. All are expecting something to happen there any day. There are thousands of Turks thirty miles off the Canal and our men letting them gather as many as they can, and then into them with our cavalry. They are real cowards when charged and then they might get better results, as the Dardanelles. Our position is none too safe there, for there are hundreds of Greeks and Bedouin waiting to mobilize and there are zeppelins which could drop bombs on our camps, of course. They can't fly past ours at the Canal yet, but still on the whole things are not looking at all well.

We have not received any wounded in for some time and all hospitals are practically empty. But if this big fight comes off at Suez, well, we will get quite enough. The Turks are going to try and get the railway from Suez to Cairo. But of course they have more work to do. Rollie has gone back, Mother. He did not look fit but he would go. I feel very sad and lonely. He wrote me a beautiful letter and gave (it to) me when we said goodbye. I hope he will be alright. He was four and a half months in the trenches before, so perhaps he will keep lucky.

It is such a risk going over now. That submarine is about and stray mines too. If his mother and sister arrive, I will meet them. He got his photo taken but it is not a bit nice. However I shall send you one of them. I am dying to hear if you like my photos and hope you get the parcel. The brass coffee set is real Egyptian make and the tent work is nice to tack on the wall at the back of the washstands. The donks *(donkeys)* are funny, aren't they? The little gong is used here very much. I just sent them so as to have something from Egypt. I can't afford to get anything very expensive.

One of our Sisters came back from Transport last night. She went as far as Sydney and brought back heaps of parcels, mostly cakes for the girls from their people. Sister Dunn came back. She was the first Queensland sister to return with the wounded to Brisbane. They seemed to have made a great fuss of her too. They wouldn't see my heels for dust trying to catch the train for Gladstone, to catch the boat for Townsville.

Well Mum, Denis Walker is still up at the Palace. I go and see him. He has been a long time over on the peninsula and had not had any letters from home for weeks, and you know how they write to him. The poor boys, their letters never get to them. I sent little packets of cigarettes often to Bill Cowton and a few others. I wonder do they get them. Hope you have a bright Christmas, don't think it will be very merry anywhere.

Love to you all.

Xxxxxx Queenie.

P.S. Am afraid Christmas dinner will be on the boat, near Sydney somehow. Q.

Editor's Note: This particular Christmas, my father and his brother received one little polished apple and a little Union Jack for presents in Townsville. Thereafter any Christmas presents in our family had to be an improvement.

Pat Richardson

Chapter 5: Transport Duty and Home

No. 1 Australian General Hospital, Heliopolis,
6th November, 1915.

Dearest Mother and family,

The mail closes tomorrow and I have just received a notice from headquarters to say I am to go on the next transport for Australia. It may be this week and perhaps in three weeks, but I will be on my way back soon. Now, in Sydney I shall wire you when I arrive if you would like to come down to Brisbane and stay the fortnight with me. I can wire you the money quite easily, otherwise I can come up and we'll have a few days with you only. You may only get this letter a few days before we arrive in Sydney. You can send all messages to Coley.

I can easily wire you the fare, Mum, and the change would do you good. Coley has a lovely cottage at Redcliffe and we could be together. Jim could "batch" at home with Len, and Bob could go down to Doll's. Otherwise I can come up to see you all, only it seems selfish of me to spend the fare on myself when you could have the benefit of the money. It is my little hoard I have kept by me in case I was in need of money. I cannot afford to spend another piastre here.

Of course, Mother this may not come off, but you can expect a wire from me anytime after receiving this. One never knows what we are going to do in the military. I would love to bring home the wounded. I must stop, only have a few minutes so thought you would like some notice.

Love to you all.

xxxxx Queenie.

Editor's note: At this point in her army service, Queenie had been nursing at Heliopolis since 29th June, 1915. She has had two weeks leave in Australia and is now on way back to Egypt. She embarked on HMAT Borda from Suez on November 15, with leave from 13th December, 1915. The Queenslander of January 8th, 1916, ran the following gossip piece from its Townsville correspondent: "Sister Avenel (sic) *of the Australian Hospital, Cairo, who has been spending a week with her parents, left on Monday to rejoin her hospital ship. The Brisbane Courier of January 1st noted: "Sister Edith Avenell of No. 1 Australian General Hospital, is staying with Mrs J.F. Cole, Elswick, Enoggera, and expects to return to England shortly."*

At sea, on the return to Egypt,
18th February, 1916.

Dear Mother,

Our engines broke down so we are late getting to Colombo. All one night we were not moving. A pipe burst in the boiler and they had to empty it before putting in a new one. We are having fine weather and the sea today is just like a pond; hardly a ripple in it. I am writing this in hospital and there is great excitement outside. The men are having sports. Eight times round the deck is a mile, so they are now running off in heats, all the different reinforcements backing their own. Great competition with them all.

News is very dull and the time gets a bit monotonous; we will all be glad to get off the boat. This transport is a palace to the one I came out on, really. The Sisters have very cool and comfortable cabins. It was very cold at first, but now it is just the other extreme coming to Colombo. Expect to cross the Line tomorrow, hope it won't bump the ship too much!

We have another stowaway on board. I believe if Len was in any way near the camps, he would be away like these youngsters; they mean to get over there. We have ten patients in now, some are pretty bad too – mostly pneumonia and colds. We work one week and off the next. My week on now. They had another concert last night. I am doing a grey pair of socks now. Finished one, and on the other. I knit the proper way too. It is very fascinating work. I have nearly embroidered a nightie for myself, too. Read plenty of books. Some rather good ones for the Red Cross. Well, so long till next day. Q.

20th February, 1916. Arriving Colombo tomorrow so will say "Au revoir", tons of love and kisses to you all in Townsville and Mackay.

Queenie.

At sea, on the return to Egypt,
2nd March, 1916.

Dearest Mother and all at home,

We are within four days now of our destination, and we all feel sorry it is so near, for it has been most enjoyable. The weather, perfect. We stayed a day and a half in Colombo, and had dinner at the Galle Face Hotel. I was on night duty so came back to the boat about eleven o'clock, and as there was nothing to do I got into a chair and slept all night.

Then the next day Major Argyle and myself took a boat over to the Hospital ship "Nestor", which came into the harbour previous day. I met several sisters from "Luna Park" and also patients. We had lunch with them and came back an hour before leaving Colombo. All the troops went ashore in two different lots, had a route march, then dismissed for a couple of hours. Some did not return that night and the O.C. had to send out guards to bring them in. Tom Cole was one of them, but of course, don't tell Coley. He was "tight" *(drunk)* and did not know where he was, had a real good old time, though.

I had a lovely white crepe-de-chine silk scarf given me by one of the troops. He saw me at the hotel, so went into the silk shop and gave it me. I do not possess a decent one, so it is very handy and it is worked beautifully. I must send you a black sequin one from Egypt, too. I bought a little ivory ornament for one rupee myself, otherwise that is all I got. The girls bought some very pretty "kims" *(kimonos)* but Rollie told me he was going to get me one, so I did not bother.

The men are such grand fellows. We still have the (ship's) hospital full, but it has only fifteen beds and that's not many for twelve hundred people. Yesterday was our most interesting day so far. We passed Aden, light houses, and ships all day, armed merchant vessels, and a small cruiser. The sea is still a green and blue colour and very calm. This morning our Marconi picked up a message stating the "Maloja" has been sunk with two hundred passengers off Gibraltar. I saw that boat coming into Fremantle as we came out on our way home. We are to have a lifeboat drill in the middle of the night.

We hear such a lot of rumours in Colombo. The No.3 General Hospital is in Cairo from Lemnos. Echlin and Gibbon have gone to Australia on transport. Sister Grant has had typhoid but is up again. Gordon House where we all live from Luna Park is closed down and we are messing at the Palace. There are over a quarter of a million soldiers in Egypt, and lots of bull and gossip.

I am looking forward to seeing Rollie. I heard his regiment is still in Cairo, so expect he will meet me at the station. It will be four months since we parted so it be a cheero. I have knitted another pair of socks for him. Have not any more news I can think of just now, but will add more to this later. I dreamt I was married last night and you were at the wedding, it was all military too so that is a good omen for me and I believe I will too. So long for a while. xxxxx

4th March, 1916. Disembarking tomorrow Mum, so we are very busy packing up. Heaps of love, kisses to you all.

Queenie.

No. 3 General Hospital, Abbassia,
28th March, 1916.

Dearest Mother and boys and Family,

I am off in the morning for France, rejoining my unit again, so you can address my letters to No. 1 A.G.H. C/- Intermediate Base. They will always forward them to us. I was so surprised to be taken, but the unit was reorganised, so that is why I am going back.

Everything seems to turn out for the best, for Rollie came up last Saturday from away down the Canal, a place called Serapeum, near Ismalia, (and) stayed the day and night. He is a Lieutenant, and his brother came up from his regiment too. He is in the New Zealanders, and got wounded on the landing at the peninsula, went home to England and married his cousin, an only child, plenty of tin *(money)*. So he was very lonely. He was only a corporal then, but is an officer now.

He was very jealous of Rollie and me, but we cheered him up. His wife is home in England, but we are all moving out of Egypt. Rollie hopes to be going in the next few weeks. We are going to a hospital in Boulogne, ten thousand beds, fancy, Mother, what an experience for me. I hope we shall get to England and I can see Aunty.

I have not had any mail from you since I left Brisbane but I s'pose it's here somewhere. Just got six letters, two from you dated February 7th and the 17th. Sorry to hear poor old Doll is not well. I do wish she would stop having those children; they are dear things, but still she is very young and could have kiddies in ten years hence, if she was careful. I don't know much about those sort of things, but I do know she could be careful. They are too much for her to look after and a mere handful herself. By golly, I'm not going to have them so soon.

Rollie is a dear old man, Mum. He says he loves me more than ever, and did miss me terribly when he came back from the peninsula. He was the last to leave the firing lines, he and eight of the troopers. I did not have half long enough with him to tell me all about everything. They are so strict with the officers and their leave.

They are all coming near us, for their camps will be wherever we are in France, so we shall see each other again soon. One half of the troops are over there by now. Every Australian will be out of Egypt before the first of June. I was so glad he is a Lieutenant and has his stars up. He is writing you a letter, Mum, and asked after you all. It is my birthday on Friday and Rollie is twenty-seven in July, just a year older than I.

The boys will be glad to get away from this dirty hole. Really I am beginning to detest the place. The smells and filth of the streets are awful. Rollie says he's glad to be on the Canal. No fighting there at all. It seems to me the war will be over in a few months. It will be great if that is so. I am afraid Rollie and I won't be able to get married till we come back, so you will have me stepping out of our little house in our uniforms. Roll and I had a good old talk about it, but anything might happen. Might be left behind, for they will have some heavy fighting to do in France.

We are all very excited about going away. *(Nurses)* Grant, Chidgey and Kemp are left here as they came out so much later. They are furious at not going with us. Well, Mum, I will write you again next week. Hope you are getting all my letters. I have written you five in the last three weeks since we arrived.

Heaps of love to you all and kisses for all.

Queenie xxxx

Ghurkas. It is an Indian word for home. The pats don't stay long in these hosp. as they improve they get sent to the base hosps in England. They get grand treatment & attention in the hospitals. They deserve it all of course for there are some fearful cases. I don't know how they live. This place is pretty but deadly just now. Can't go anywhere & never out at night. In absolute darkness all the time. Last night we got warning for an air raid but

No 13th Stationary
Boulogne
14.5.16

Dearest Mother

I think I have written to you since I've been on night duty however it's a week today & has passed quickly. You know how I loathe night duty & I'm on for two months fancy. & in the busiest ward of the hosp. We receive convoys every other night. I had two Aust. in my ward but they went to 'Blighty' today. Blighty means home. & the Tommies of course are always talking of going to blighty. It originated from the

it didn't come off. never does we often get word. It is very depressing in France we all get down to zero. I suppose it is living the whole time with war surrounding really Mother I don't know what will become of it all — I want to get back to Aust. the moment it is all over. not a bit anxious to see England although on clear days. Dover is seen quite easily from here.

I'm full up of war & everything. No one seems to be missed in the lines so I am not thinking too much about Rollie. Funny how we had got married in Egypt. & else never met at all. He is so careless under fire too. his men have told me that. he's had good luck so far. You know he was recommended for the D.C.M. for being the last to leave the peninsular but have not heard since whether he got it. I've not had a letter since I left Egypt.

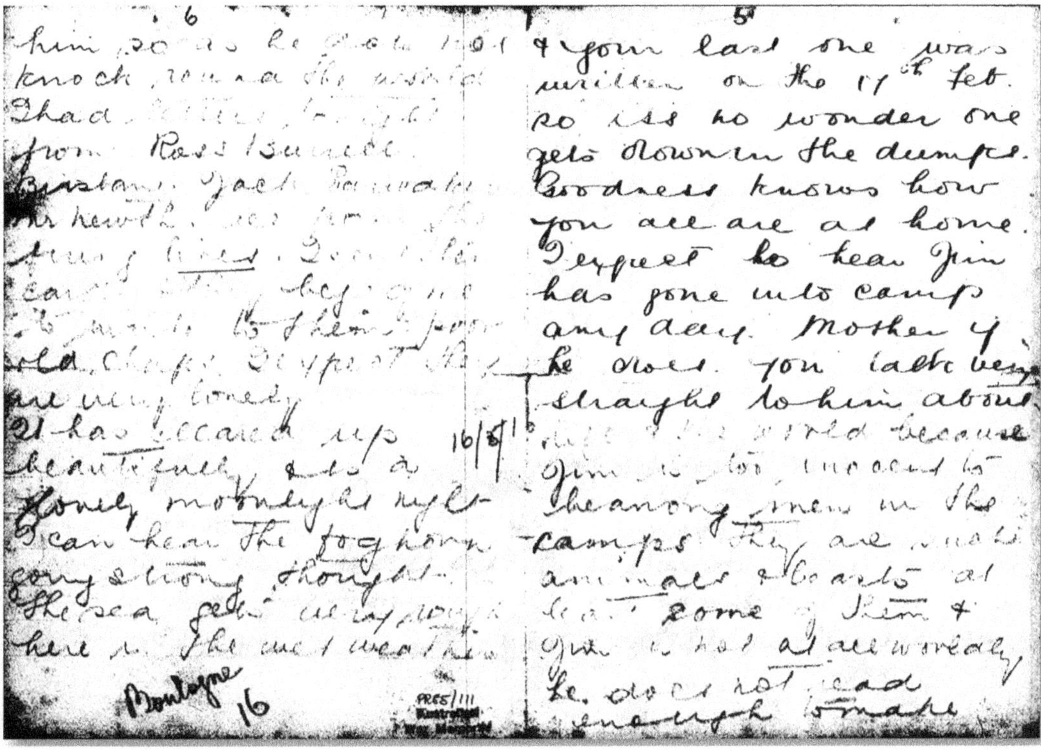
5
& your last one was
written on the 17th Feb.
so it is no wonder one
gets down in the dumps.
Goodness knows how
you all are at home.
I expect to hear Jim
has gone into camp
any day. Mother if
he does you talk very
straight to him about
all the world because
Jim is too innocent to
be among men in the
camps. They are [illegible]
animals & brutes at
least some of them &
Jim is not at all worldly
he does not read
enough to make
6
him so as he does not
knock round the world
I had letters tonight
from [illegible]
[illegible]
[illegible]
[illegible]
[illegible]
[illegible]
old chaps. I expect they
are very lonely.
It has cleared up 16/8/16
beautifully & it's a
lovely moonlight night.
I can hear the foghorn
going strong though.
The sea gets very rough
here in the wet weather.
Boulogne 16
PRES/111

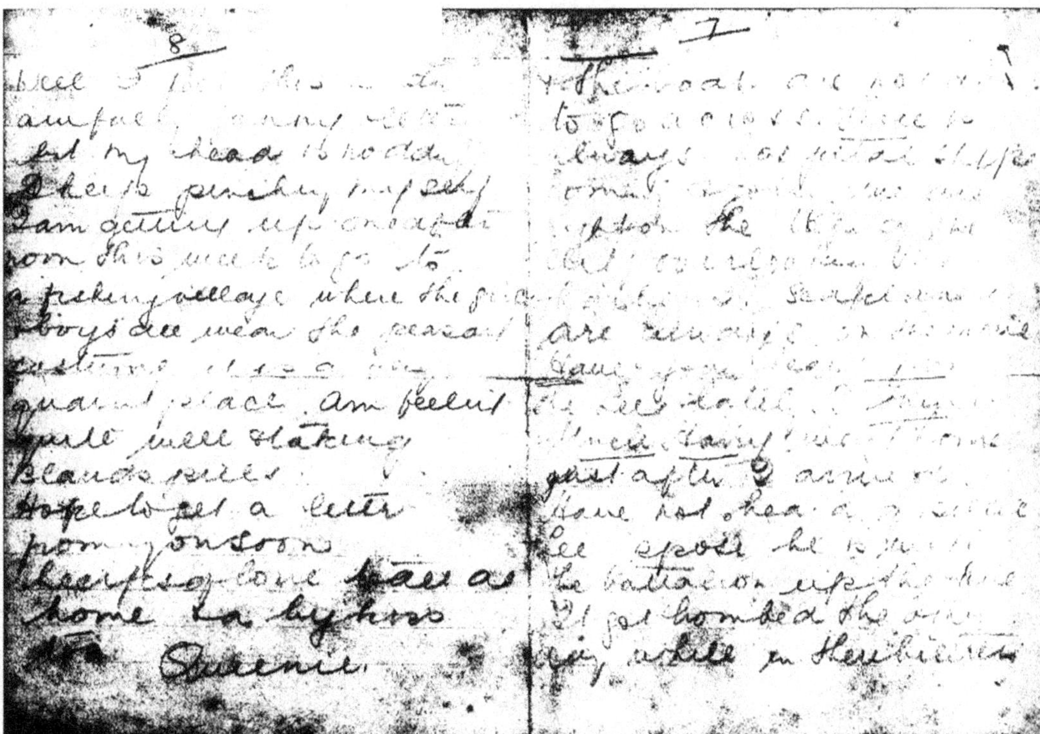
7
& the roads are [illegible]
to go across. There is
always [illegible]
[illegible]
[illegible]
[illegible]
[illegible]
are always [illegible]
[illegible]
[illegible]
Uncle Harry [illegible]
just after I arrived.
Have not heard [illegible]
[illegible]
the battalion [illegible]
It got bombed the other
day while in the billets.
8
well [illegible]
am [illegible]
but my head is nodding.
I keep pinching myself.
I am getting up early afternoon this week to go to
a fishing village where the girls &
boys all wear the peasant
costume. It is a very
quaint place. Am feeling
quite well & taking
Blaud's pills.
Hope to get a letter
from you soon.
Heaps of love to all at
home & a big kiss
from Queenie

Chapter 6: France

Only two letters remain from Queenie's six-month service in France. She was in the habit of writing every week, but many letters home were lost when ships were sunk or, if they arrived safely, would be passed around family members and mislaid, lost to history – and, sadly, to a generation of Australians now rediscovering the women like Queenie and her colleagues, many mentioned in these letters, who comforted, healed and grieved over the human detritus of war.

Queenie sailed into Marseilles harbour with her unit, No. 1 Australian General Hospital, on April 5th, 1916, the hospital ship Salta waiting in the shipping roads for a day before being cleared to dock alongside the quay the following morning. Unloading an entire general hospital was a major operation. On board was a staff of twenty medical officers, a dental officer, three chaplains, the quartermaster, three masseurs and one hundred and fifteen nurses. Also packed and ready to leave the vessel were three dental details, four motor drivers and one hundred and eight-seven "other ranks". The Salta was sunk the following year when she sailed into a German minefield off Le Havre with the loss of one hundred and thirty nurses, wounded and crew.

Transport attached to the hospital comprised one motor touring car, a motor ambulance, a motor lorry and two motor cycles. The equipment tallied eight hundred and fifty tons, excluding tents and was enough for a seven hundred and fifty-bed hospital capable of expanding to one thousand beds. The hospital also had its own x-ray, dental and pathology departments. From early in the morning the quayside was a hive of organised activity as the vehicles, operating tables, tents, carefully packed instruments, medicines and sundry other equipment were unloaded and stored in sheds on the quay.

At midday the following day, the officers and other ranks disembarked and were taken to the military camp at Carcasonne, but it was not until April 8th that the nurses left the ship. Their orders were to travel to Rouen by train, with the full complement of hospital stores and equipment, where they arrived on April 12th. No. 1 AGH was set up in tents on the town's racecourse, but almost immediately it was decided most of the nurses were not needed yet, and one hundred and seventeen were seconded to British units in Le Havre, Boulogne, Etaples and Le Treport, with a further fifty dispersed to other British hospitals in Rouen. From a single entry in the unit diary for April 1916, it appears Sister Edith Avenell stayed on the Rouen racecourse.

A frenetic fortnight of unloading the train and setting up the hospital later, and 1AGH was reported ready to receive patients on April 29th, staffed by the full complement of medical officers who had disembarked from the Salta, plus forty-seven of their forty-eight nursing staff. Just eleven patients were admitted – this was to change dramatically within a few weeks. Eight days earlier on 21st April, according to an entry in the unit diary, one nurse "departed to hospital". On that date, according to her army service record held at the National Archives of Australia, Queenie was sent to No. 14 General Hospital in Wimereux, suffering from pyrexia, a severe fever. Discharged on May 4, she was to serve briefly with No. 13 Stationary Hospital in Boulogne before returning to her unit with No. 1 AGH on July 4.

The single letter she wrote to her mother from France was during her time in Boulogne, where she describes the nurses as "living all the time with war surrounding". The hospital was close to the front line and convoys of wounded with horrific injuries – smashed limbs, faces half shot away, great shrapnel gouges and always the creeping, deadly infection that often overtook medical staff before they could mend the shattered bodies of men who were once whole and strong – were constants against the backdrop of screaming shells, exploding ordnance and the rumble of convoys to the front with more men to be returned broken, bleeding and traumatised by the killing fields of France. It was far worse than Galllipoli.

Of the racecourse hospital at Rouen, First World War medical historian Colonel Graham Butler wrote: "During the AIF's first year in France (1916) the nurses, especially at Rouen, had a very hard time indeed. This hospital had not been equipped, as were the British, with stoves; and coming fresh from Egypt it was quite unprepared for the rigours of Europe." Through the three years the hospital operated at Rouen, ninety thousand cases passed through its wards, mostly from the Somme battles.

No. 13 Stationary Hospital, Boulogne,
14th May, 1916.

Dearest Mother,

I think I have written to you since I've been on night duty, however it's a week today and has passed quickly. You know how I loathe night duty and I'm on for two months, fancy, in the busiest ward of the hospital. We receive convoys every other night. I had two Australians in my ward but they went to "Blighty" *(England)* today. Blighty means home, and the Tommies, of course, are always talking of going to Blighty. It originated from the Ghurkas, and is an Indian word for "home".

The patients don't stay long in these hospitals; as they improve they get sent to the base hospitals in England. They get grand treatment and attention in the hospitals. They deserve it all of course, for there are some fearful cases. I don't know how they live. This place is pretty, but deadly just now. Can't go anywhere and never out at night; in absolute darkness all the time. Last night we got warning for an air raid but it didn't come off. Never does, we often get word.

It is very depressing in France. We all get down to zero. I suppose it is living the whole time with war surrounding. Really, Mother, I don't know what will become of it all; I want to get back to Australia the moment it is all over. Not a bit anxious to see England although on clear days, Dover is seen quite easily from here. I'm fed up of war and everything.

No one seems to be missed in the lines so I am not thinking too much about Rollie. I wish now we had got married in Egypt, or else never met at all. He is so careless under fire too. His men have told me that he's had good luck so far. You know he was recommended for the D.C.M. *(Distinguished Conduct Medal)* for being the last to leave the peninsula, but have not heard since whether he is to get it.

I've not had a letter since I left Egypt and your last one was written on 17th February, so it's no wonder one gets down in the dumps. Goodness knows how you are all at home. I expect to hear Jim has gone into camp any day. Mother, if he does, you talk very straight to him about life and the world, because Jim is too innocent to be among men in the camps. They are such animals and beasts, (at least some of them) and Jim is not at all worldly. He does not read enough to make him so, as he does not knock round the world.

I had letters tonight from Ross Burrell, Jack Earwaker and Mr Newth, all from the firing lines. I sent them cards and they beg of me to write to them. Poor old chaps, I expect they are very lonely. It has cleared up beautifully and is a lovely moonlight night. I can hear the foghorn going strong, though the sea gets very rough here in the wet weather and the boats are not able to go across. There are always hospital ships coming and going, we are right on the top of the cliff overlooking the harbour. Seaplanes are always on the move.

Have you heard from the Lees lately? I think Uncle Harry went home just after I arrived. Have not heard of Billie Lee, s'pose he is with the battalion up the line. It got bombed the other day while in billets. Well I feel this is an awfully funny letter but my head is nodding. I keep pinching myself. I am getting up one afternoon this week to go to a fishing village where the girls and boys all wear the peasant costume. It is a very quaint place. Am feeling quite well and taking Blands pills.

Hope to get a letter from you soon. Heaps of love to all at home and a big kiss too.

Queenie.

The second letter to survive from Queenie's six months service in France was to a family friend, Padre David Garland, who was serving with No. 6 Australian General Hospital in Brisbane.

In 1902, the Padre had been rector of the Anglican Church at Charters Towers in far north Queensland and was later the Archdeacon of North Queensland. He held leading positions within the diocese over the following few years, including registrar from 1904 to 1907, when he was based in Townsville at St James Anglican Cathedral. Born in Dublin in 1864, he died in Brisbane in 1939. The Avenells were at Clermont and Bowen during this time and, as practising Anglicans they would have been acquainted with him. Queenie's mother, Matilda, received a letter from the rector at Clermont, thanking her for running a concert for the church during race week in July 1906.

Padre Garland enlisted to serve in the First World War and from 1914 to 1917 was Senior Army Camp Chaplain in Queensland. He served overseas from 1917 to 1918 in the Middle East with Australian troops, and celebrated the first Eucharist in the Church of the Holy Sepulchre in Jerusalem after the expulsion of the Turks.

After the war, Padre Garland initiated the Anzac Day March, the Returned Soldiers Luncheon and the two minutes silence, worked for many charitable endeavours and was awarded many honours. He is listed in the Australian Dictionary of Biography.

No. 13 Stationary Hospital, Boulogne,
8th June, 1916.

Dear Padre,

I received your letter and little cross last week for which I thank you. I am sorry I have not written sooner I've been in France. I have very little time even to write to mother once a week. The sisters are splendid the way they work, our hours are fearfully long. From 7.a.m. till 8.p.m.,day duty, and 7.p.m to 8.a.m., night duty. I am doing the latter, but I should really be sleeping, but I can't today.

We had a big convoy in last night – shocking cases. I simply ran for ten solid hours without a stop, and then the news of Kitchener *(General Kitchener, Secretary of State for War, was lost at sea when on board the cruiser Hampshire when it hit a mine after leaving Scapa Flow, off the North of Scotland).* That upset me. It's bewildering we can't realize it yet, we are all in mourning for him, and there is to be a memorial service for him, the King and Queen being present.

Boulogne is rather interesting, and, of course, very historical. I have not had the energy to go out to some of the villages, but this hospital is on the spot where Napoleon and his troops were camped and preparing to invade England. There is a monument in the grounds. We can see Dover Castle this morning from my bedroom window, so you see we are right up on the cliff.

Our troops are only one hour's motor ride away, but we never see them, only when they are on leave – the leave boats and mail boats go every day across to Southampton accompanied by the Silver King and Queen *(airships)* and also destroyers. This hospital is all surgical and I can't find Tom Cole anywhere, have written to different addresses but I'm sure he's transferred. Jack has not heard of him either. I do hope he's alright. I did like Mr Paul coming over on the "Wondilla". He was fearfully miserable leaving his little wife behind. Mr Marty looked after us very well, we called him "Father". They were an awfully nice lot of boys, too. I used to be with them all day.

Well I'm sorry to hear such scandal discussed about the sisters. The only sister I knew got sent back was because she married without the C.O.'s permission. Otherwise sisters here are having a trying time. Of course it was different in Egypt – we did go out and had a gay time when off duty during the latter part of our stay there, but why shouldn't we? It gave our troops pleasure to be with us and much better for them than down the town with bad company. I think some people are jealous of the sisters being out here with the troops. We never go out here, but are glad to drop into bed when off duty. I'm afraid after two years of it I will have to give it up for a while.

Well I really must try to sleep. Before closing I must thank you for being kind to my mother. A few years ago we would have been too proud to think of such a thing. Times change, and so farewell for the present. Best Wishes,

Yours Sincerely,

Edith Avenell.

P.S. I am wearing my cross. Hope you are still looking after the boys in camp as the troops on the boats told me about you and said very nice things too.

This letter was sent to me by the late Mrs Gwen Robinson of Mt Gravatt, Brisbane. She wrote a book based on the Letters and Diaries of our nurses in the First World War, called "The Forgotten Women".

Pat Richardson

Chapter 7: To England

The grim parade of broken, sick and dying men sent Queenie into a downward spiral of depression and anxiety, culminating in a nervous breakdown in September, 1916. At the beginning of that month, the campsite hospital on the Rouen racecourse held one thousand, one hundred beds. The patient numbers that month, from the daily count in the unit diary, fluctuated between thirty-two and seven hundred and seventeen.

During this month alone, three thousand, nine hundred and twenty-one men were admitted for an average stay each of just under three days. Most were evacuated to English hospitals, with eighty-eight transferred to other hospitals in France, eight hundred and one sent to convalescent camps and one hundred and eighteen sent to duty bases. There were thirty-eight deaths. Nine hundred and ninety-seven operations were performed by a staff whose numbers, depending on movements and needs elsewhere, as well as staff illnesses, fluctuated between nine and twenty-three medical officers and seventy and seventy-four nurses.

On 27th September, after working long hours, seven days a week for six months without a break, Queenie was granted what we would now call stress leave and was sent to England. She was suffering from neurasthenia – colloquially known as "shell shock" and today called post-traumatic stress disorder. At its most severe, symptoms range from disorientation and hysteria to delusion and even limb paralysis and loss of speech. The medical board Queenie attended in England in October, 1916, about a fortnight after her arrival from France, noted: "She is sleeping badly and is very nervous and apprehensive of being able to carry on in France. Since arriving to England, she has slept better and has been less nervous".

She was sent to a nursing home in St Albans for fourteen days' recuperation and later seconded to No. 2 Australian Auxiliary Hospital at Southall for what were known as light duties – which would have constituted a full day's work today. Hating the thought of returning to France, she tells her mother she will try and obtain a transfer to an English hospital, because "... Mum, if I don't look after myself, no-one else will".

Meanwhile, with her typical common sense, Queenie determines to see London and enjoy herself while she can.

Glenalmond, St. Albans, Hertfordshire, England,
29th September, 1916.

Mum Dear,

As you note the address I really am in England at last. Matron sent me off "toute de suite" the day before yesterday, and I arrived here yesterday at midday. Left Rouen 7 p.m. the night before. I am in bed, but only for rest for a few days. Am not ill at all, so don't worry because I tell you I am in bed. This is simply glorious coming to a home and a bed.

I am rather bewildered at the comfort around me and can't realize I am away from active service in France yet. It seems to have a depressing feeling with me or perhaps it is the reaction, but I have just cried since I came and it is so silly too. You know I never howl, but I am not so bad today. Yesterday after I had a hot bath and got into bed, my meals brought to me and everybody so kind, I felt it was really too much for me. However I'm here for a whole fortnight so I am going to rest the first week and then go up to London for a couple of days before I go back. I am trying not to think of that part. I just loathe the thought of going back and will have to buy warm clothes to last the winter.

A real English Colonel looked after me all the way over. I came down to Le Havre by the Paris mail train, and then got the packet. Slept in a berth all night, the boat hardly moved going over and we got into Southampton at 9 a.m. where we caught the train to Waterloo Station. I had to report to Miss *(Evelyn)* Conyers, our Matron-In-Chief, at the Australian Base Horseferry Road, and then said "Au revoir" to my good friend. He was very nice and rather a big "hit" as he owns an ammunition factory over here, and had been to Verdun to see his own shells in action and on military business. However, he was awfully kind to me.

The Matron here is one of our nurses from No. 1 A.G.H., so she says it's not right to keep us over in France longer than three months, without a week's rest at least. Well, I'm going to try and forget all the horror I've left behind and enjoy myself. I saw the great Netley Hospital on the right coming into Southampton waters. Echlin is there, but she hates it – too many military rules.

(May be a page missing, as it is not signed)

Glenalmond, St. Albans, Hertfordshire,
30th September, 1916.

Well, Mum, I wrote this all last night. This morning's mail is a letter from my Colonel's wife asking me to come and stay at their flat next week and go gay for a night or two. What hospitable people, eh? I don't think I shall accept the invitation; I do not feel equal to it and besides I expect Rollie any moment. He is over in Ireland with his people and is coming back "toute de suite". But it is kind of these people to look after we Australians.

I must send you a book, "Love Letters of an Anzac", and my Rollie's name in it twice. Oliver Hogue was a Sergeant with Rollie in the old 6th Light Horse, and Morrell, Moffat, Alford and Smithy are all his pals. Of course, since Rollie has his commission he is in the 56th Battalion Imperial transferred. He would still be in Egypt, otherwise, with the Light Horse.

They *(Love Letters of an Anzac)* are awfully nice, and so true as we all know in a minute; I almost wish you could read it now. Wasn't it funny, I felt too hysterical to think of reading while in bed, and the first book I picked up was this, so it did me good reading old times.

St. Albans, from my bedroom window, looks a garden of flowers, with lovely old homes. I can hear the chimes of the Abbey now, and there are some wonderful old ruins not far away, but all this for me when I have rested, feel ever so much better since yesterday.

Sister Webb from Brisbane is in my room; she has had German measles and is here for a month. She is such a brick, and has cheered me up wonderfully already. I was up out of bed in my nightie last night trying on her mufti hats, if you please, and I brought over a few little neck wears from France. They look very Frenchy, you know, and they were all trying them on. When I go up to London I feel I want to go straight and get you something at once, if it's only some little collar.

The Sisters look dreadfully ill here, and yet it's really only "run-down". They call us the "Paleface Brigade", and we call the English girls the "pink and whites". They are awfully pretty, I hear, and I'm just achy to get out now and see them. Well, Mum, I will write to you again in a day or two.

Much love to you all. I think of you all the time.

xxxxx Queenie

Glenalmond, St. Albans, Hertfordshire,
3rd October, 1916.

Dear Mum,

Just a few lines to you all as I am sitting up in the billiard room like Jacky and a real "Lidy" with nothing to do and comfort all around me. A nice fire too, so I always feel I want to write and tell you all this. Have not been up to London yet, but I am going to see Miss Conyers, our Matron-In-Chief, and ask her to try and keep me in London or some part of England. I don't want to go back to France. I hate the thought of convoys and evacuations.

Yesterday I went down to the town of St. Albans, walked through paddocks or fields they call them, over stiles and passed an old inn called "The Fighting Cock", it is the oldest inhabited house in England. Saw the outside of the Abbey, where the tower part was built by the Normans. It is a beautiful part of England and this home and grounds are lovely.

Oh, but I never told you yet, I saw a zeppelin come down in a mass of flames the night before last, it lit up our room and we rushed out of bed and just saw it in time. It is about ten miles from here hanging from a tree (one part of it). The aeroplane that brought it down was near it, and kept throwing out different coloured lights signalling. It was most exciting, all the people cheering and singing.

They say the cries of the men were awful as the zeppelin came down. Some threw themselves out; of course, they were dead and all burnt. Really isn't it dreadful, they came over here with the intent to murder people and they get so daring and then are killed themselves? We thought they would come over last night but I don't think they did.

Well, I must write again in a few days. Much love and kisses to you all.

xxxxx Queenie

Hotel Windsor, Victoria Street, Westminster,
October, 1916.

Dearest Mum and all at home,

I am on leave and staying here for a few days. Was going up to Scotland, but waiting until later when winter is over. I got quite a surprise when I was told to go on a fortnight's furlough, so my word, I took it, you see. The fortnight I had at St. Albans was sick leave. I thought it was counted as furlough.

Well, Mum I went through Westminster Abbey and St. Margaret's Church which, of course, is dedicated to Colonials. I don't know if they use it very much, but I had a good look at it all. Am sorry I won't see Andy as I've just got your letter saying he is coming over and going to Aldershot. Well, it's hard luck because I want to go down there with Uncle next week. He can show me all over it. Andy will be lucky having Uncle right there, won't he?

I am going to stay with Auntie *(Emily Palmer, relatives living in London, previously Emily Avenell)* for a few days. Of course, three of us are here together. Any amount of Australians I know. Three Colonels, (Dawson and Hooper), they all look after me. Colonel Dawson took us to the Tower of London, saw the Crown Jewels and all the historic parts, armouries, scaffolds, etc. I also went one morning to Madame Tussaud's. Great isn't it? I like the celebrities best in the first room. Quite puzzled sometimes which ones were the wax figures. They were splendid, Lloyd George, Churchill, French Joffre, Kitchener, etc., they were very real.

So you see I'm doing the sights. Have been to several theatres: "Peg O' My Heart", and this afternoon I went to "The Professor's Love Story", H.B. Irving being the Professor, at the Savoy, this was. Captain Foxlee took me out to lunch and the theatre after. We did love it. I know his wife, you remember. Colonel Hooper told him to look after me. It's funny how we meet people over here in such a big place. Oh, I did love Peg, she was so clever. I get carried away for the time being (I don't think).

I wonder if Dolly and Ken are still in Innisfail. I will send her blouse with yours and not by any sisters this time, for you have never told me if you got that black silver scarf and it was so pretty, too. I gave it to a sister to post in Australia to you.

They say there are more people in London than there has ever been, really the crowds and crowds of people and oh, the Tube and subways. You can either take an electric underground car or go further down the bowels of the earth and take a Tube. They take you to very central spots. I have not been to any of the sights because I really am resting. I have not written to anyone so you must tell anyone enquiring for me, all the news.

Grandad is a marvel. It's about five weeks since I got a letter from you so I s'pose any mail will come over from France now. I must write to the base and get it sent here now. It's soon time for another zeppelin raid. Wasn't it funny I should see the last one all in flames gliding down? All the place is in darkness. The police were in to the girls last night for not having the blinds drawn properly. They get fined if they don't and quite right too, it's so serious. I know what I can do now, send you some papers. Get the boys to wrap them up for me.

I am meeting Bert Norris next week. I always had a weak spot for Bert. He writes regularly to me. Told me in his last letter Fred Morley from Mackay *(Town Clerk),* was over a thousand pounds behind in his accounts and also a Mr. Meger, isn't it awful? *(He was a gambler)* Mr Marryat was going on the Blackall, fruit growing for his health, he never was very strong. Bert has gone over to France today with a draft of me and returns on Monday coming up to London on Tuesday and Wednesday, so will he have a gay time.

I had a very nice day in London last week with a medical officer I knew in Egypt. We had lunch at the Waldorf Hotel and went to a Matinee "The Happy Day" and then came back for five o'clock tea. The girls tangoed and ragged round the tables in the Wintergarden.

All very nice, but, oh, if we were only in Australia.

Much love to you all from

Queenie.

Chapter 8: Southall

No. 2 Australian Auxiliary Hospital,
Southall, Middlesex,
20th October, 1916.

Dearest Mum and all at home,

I am quite settled down here now, and have such lots to tell you. I wrote to Auntie and she and Will came down at once to see me. I had gone to the theatre with the patients (light duties), but they waited till 7 p.m. for me. Auntie is such a dot and carry one, *(very tiny)* and Will is not a bit tall. He is not small, but still by his photo he looks taller.

Well, we had a great old yarn and they got back at 11 p.m. Yesterday, Matron gave me the day off, so I went out to Auntie's. Went first to Broadway Ealing by train from here, then underground car to Mansion House, change, and on to the Inner Circle still underground to Liverpool Street, where I got the train to Ilford. Isn't it marvellous the way one can travel? I was exactly two hours right across London and all on my own, too.

Will met me at the station. Rene was home and little Dorothy, she is four years old and such a sweet little thing. Rene is awfully nice and is sending you a photo. We had a very nice day. Dorothy Palmer *(Dorothy Palmer, granddaughter of William Palmer, second husband of Emily Avenell)* came home from school and oh dear, she wouldn't let me out of her sight and plays and sings well for her age – ten. She is such a chatterbox, but Auntie, she talks and laughs really. We did wish you were there. Auntie is taking me down to Aldershot later and to see Kate somebody, her cousin. Uncle is a Lieutenant at Aldershot and comes home weekends so I have not met him yet.

You would know all these people better than I do, but I'm glad I've met them. I think I will be here for some time. Oh, I spent Wednesday with Bert Norris. I have not been into the wards here today, just doing odd jobs for Matron, etc. so I was up in town with Bert. He is very fond of me, Mum, it's a pity he did not tell me eight years ago, although I have always had an idea. He told me he went on that trip home to England, when he came back I was engaged to Ned Lyons. I don't know what to do. He is going to France any day. Salisbury Plains is away down Southampton way you know.

Rollie went back to France a fortnight ago, but is coming up to London again tomorrow, so I am going to a theatre with him: "The Bing Boys". I am feeling so

Selection of photos from the Australian Auxiliary Hospital, Southall during the First World War. Reprinted with the kind permission of Dr. Jonathon Oates, local historian, Ealing Broadway Library, from his book on Southall.

much better and enjoying this life, alright. The weather is getting sharp and chilly, but I like it just now. When the real cold comes, what oh, and snow too. I think this will get home to you just about Christmas time.

Well, Mum all I hope is I will be home with you all for the next. No more nursing for me then. I will tell you all about the experiences I've had, letters are very hard to write. Been on duty all day and in bed. I have one hundred and fifty-six dressings to do (on) about thirty one-armed men. Fancy, some don't need dressing every day and all are up walking about. The "legs" are in the next ward, and they are so funny, (they) show off how they can hop on the one leg and frighten the heart out of me going past them. If they should call they come on their stump. They go from here to Australia or return to the detail camps.

I have not had a letter from you for ages, but it's three weeks since I came from France, and they only knew this week I was not returning. Hope they will send them on quickly. Well, Mum, I will turn over and sleep. It's jolly cold. I won't like it when it's worse than this, but will wear plenty of flannels.

Heaps of love to you all. Trust Doll is settled alright.

xxxxx Queenie

No. 2 Australian Auxiliary Hospital,
Southall, Middlesex,
24th October, 1916.

Dear Mum,

Have been a week on duty today. It is very nice and light work, but I feel jolly fed up with nursing these days. Have not had a letter from you for about seven weeks. Isn't it dreadful the way our mail goes so long in coming? I am having a day off duty tomorrow, so I hope to spend it in town with Sister Echlin. She is at Harefield Park and came up from Netley last week.

Conscription seems to be causing a lot of strife in Australia. I have voted for it. We have got to win this war by men. I'm sick of it all and wish to goodness the war would end. Am afraid you will get this letter in a blue mood from me. Rumania by today's paper is in a bad way, which is dashed rotten for us. (The) Greek King said in fourteen days she would be wiped out, when she declared war; looks like it now doesn't it?

I sent Bob and Len a book each from Choolbreds. They are just published and very good, I think. All about the bloomin' war, of course. Fancy an old Taube *(German reconnaissance plane, originally built 1910, but superseded as a fighter plane early in 1914, Etrich-Rumpler Taube, speed 60 m.p.h.)*, coming across Margate. It's too funny to think it got there.

The leaves are all dropping and soon the trees will be bare, it is so cold now and I'm scared to think what it will be like Christmas.

Queenie and Daisy Echlin in London, November 1916. The two women kept in touch during the entire war.

I'm thinking of taking up a course of engineering with motors; it would be rather handy and I might possess a car some day. Anyhow, it only costs two guineas to learn to drive, clean and repair, which of course, I must know the whole.

I t hink there is a munitions factory close by and airships are always flying over, one is very low just now. Keeping a good watch. It must be four weeks since the last zeppelin raid. Wasn't I lucky to have seen it coming down, although I was really half asleep and could not grasp what I was looking at? I could hear the cheers of the people and the flare lit up our room. Auntie Trot is very keen on them and has quite a number of them come over their way.

I've burnt my two fingers this afternoon and they're giving me some pain – silly thing to do. Well, Mum, this letter is not very bright. Hope all are well. Would like to hear how Dolly is at Innisfail, perhaps I will get some letters tomorrow.

Much love to you all and heaps of kisses.

Queenie.

Australian Military Hospital,
Southall, Middlesex,
11th November, 1916.

Dearest Mum and all at home.

I am back here again and on duty very much so, although the work is not a bit hard, nothing to what it was like in France. I hope I won't go back there till after the winter.

Well, I thoroughly enjoyed my furlough and saw quite a lot. The last day I went to the Lord Mayor's Show. Had a seat at the Queensland office in the Strand, and was the guest of Lady Robinson, wife of the Attorney-General for Queensland. I never saw such crowds of people. The procession was military; the Anzacs looked very well, all on black horses. Of course, the chief thing to see was the Mayor in the ancient coach drawn by horses and mounted with grooms in the old fashioned dress, pink stockings and oh, such calves. The late Mayor looked jolly glad to be getting out of it. He drove in front of the new one. Colonel Dawson took me and Sister Rutledge.

I went to every theatre worth seeing. "The Best of Luck" was the best, I think. The scenery was so real and very thrilling, a motor accident, a submarine scene under water with divers and Madge Tifferidge was so sweet and clever. I love "The Professor", love story, and "Peg O' My Heart", but some of them were nothing but a lot of nonsense. "Razzle Dazzle", an awfully silly thing.

I am taking it very easy, and living quietly for a while. Auntie wanted me to stay longer with them, but I thought I had better see London as I had the chance and plenty of officers to take us anywhere. Will went back to *(text illegible, but he was at officer training school in Aldershot during this period).* After the "Arabic" *(a ship that was sunk)* they will feel rather scared. We will lose letters from you, Mum, I s'pose. I don't get many as it is, so s'pose one won't make such a difference, but it is so nice getting yours. I have read in the papers about Mr. Morley of Mackay. What a big sum!

I am hoping to take a course of lectures at a big school on motoring, the mechanism and driving, including repairs of a motor, so if I get the certificate I can always be a "chaffeuse". I have written very few letters to Australia lately. Have to answer such a number of patient's letters that I don't get time. Received a nice long letter from Vera and Daisy Richards. The latter is down on a farm in Singleton. The Father and Mother have bought it, Daisy likes it very much.

I wonder when we shall be coming home. The passengers of the "Arabic" were very cool weren't they? Fancy saving them all! It happened in the same place as that boat in front of us coming over. The weather is very smart and chilly but since I wear flannels, I don't feel the cold at all. It certainly is colder down here than in the centre of London. I will be able to tell you lots, it will bring back all your younger days to you, Mum. I can't imagine how you could have been content with such a bush existence after living in London.

(Paragraph missing)

... He has had pneumonia and his lungs are in a very bad state, a nice boy too. He used to dance with me. I have arranged with a boy in the Base Records to let me know when Andy arrives. They take such a long time coming over round the Cape (Good Hope). Well, Mum guess Christmas will be over before this reaches you. All sorts of good luck for the New Year, and I hope I will be home too.

Tons of love to you all and kisses.

xxxxxxx Queenie.

P.S. Had a nice letter from Bill Cowton; he is coming over on leave shortly.

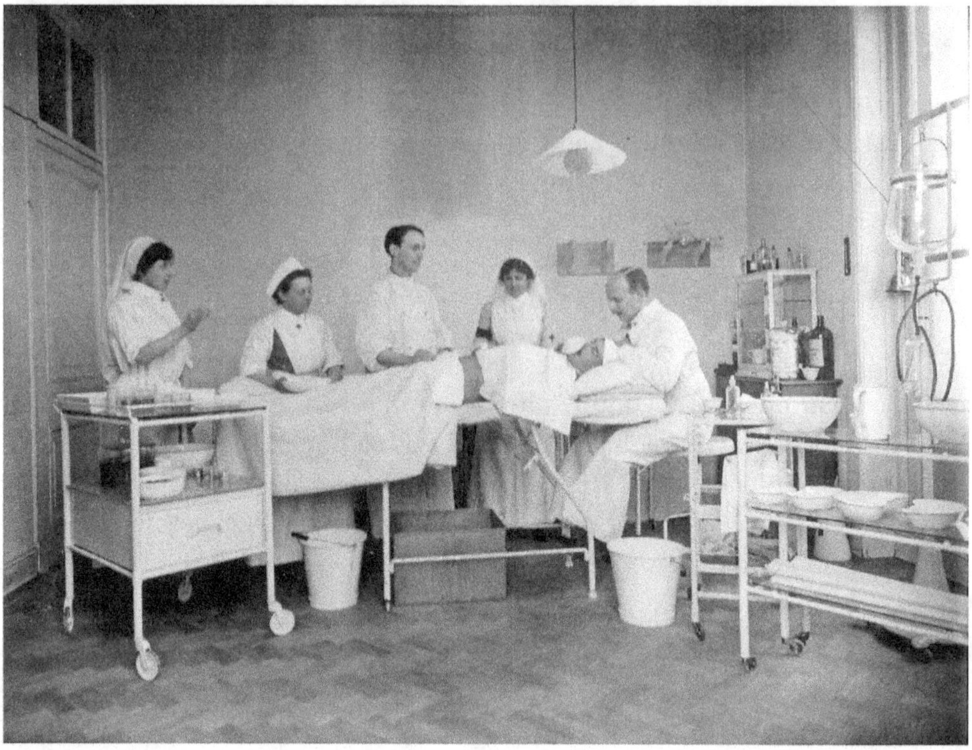

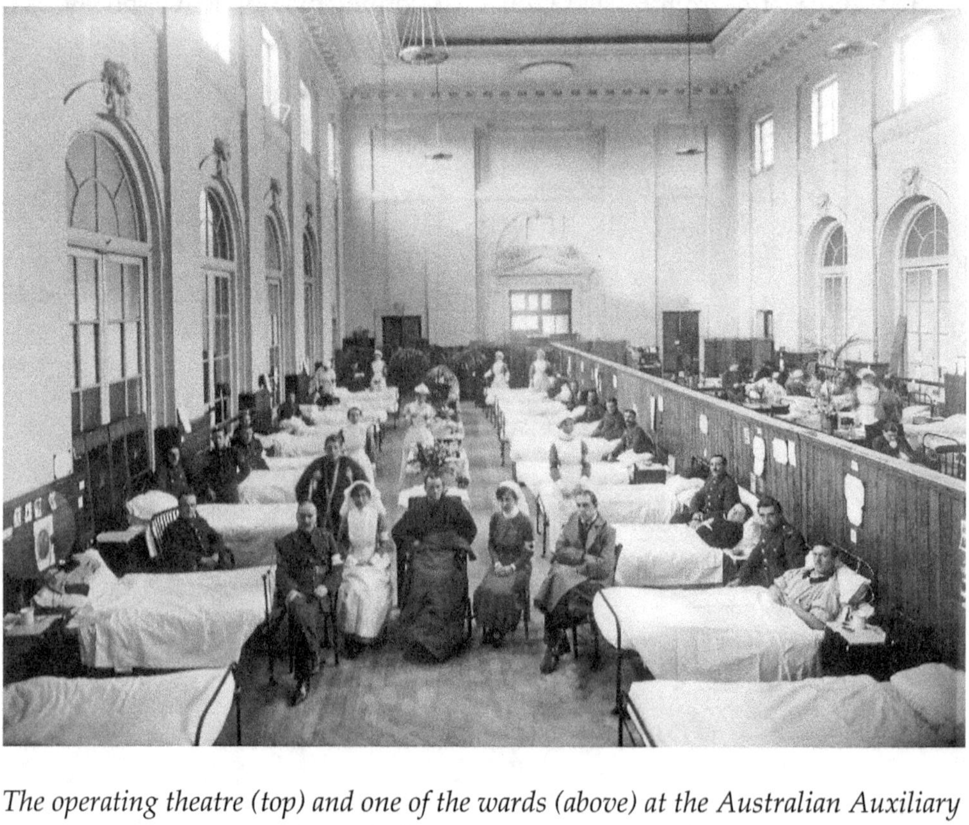

The operating theatre (top) and one of the wards (above) at the Australian Auxiliary Hospital, Southall, during the First World War.

Australian Amputee Hospital, Southall,
16th November.

Dearest Mum and all at home,

You see I have changed my address and now I am on this staff. It is a convalescent hospital and will be very light after my six months in France. I went before our medical board and they gave me two months rest, but I could not do that, so Matron said I could come here on light duties. So, I will be here in England for the winter, thank goodness.

It is heaven over here, to France. My matron over there will be furious at my not returning, but you know, Mum, if I don't look after myself no-one else will. I feel jolly run down and will take a good old rest here. I had to go in to the Base this morning, so I bought you and Doll a little white blouse each as it is summer out in Australia. I won't send anything else for Christmas, but will cable you five pounds and you can do what you like with it. Things are dearer here than in Australia, especially food. Really it's awful the price of everything.

I liked St. Albans very much. A great country life. Have written and told Auntie I'm here, so I expect she will come down or tell me how to get to her. I can't get over the size of London, it seems thousands of miles big and when I get to Trafalgar Square I get my bearings, but anywhere else I don't know whether I'm going north or south. Policemen are very good and always put you right.

I think Piccadilly Circus is lovely, the bustle and the crowd and Australians all everywhere, hundreds of them. One thousand come up on four days leave every week from Salisbury Plains, so you can guess they are everywhere, besides all the wounded men knocking round.

I went down to Norwood one day, because another Sister was going there and I took the chance of finding the Gyles', Mr Coles' sister and Mrs Len Gyle's, father and mother, they all want me to come and stay with them and are very hospitable but, of course, I can't leave the hospitals. I won't be home this year for Christmas, but will have a cold one, remember the heat last year *(in Brisbane, on furlough from Egypt).*

Australian Military Hospital, Southall,
19th November, 1916.

Dearest Mum and all at home,

Wish I could get my mail over from France soon. I am wondering if Andy has left yet and rather worried too, for he is not very quiet about his movements, name, etc. and could easily be detained, however I don't like looking on the dark side of things.

Dolly had gone back to Ayr when last you wrote. Fancy going back there to that God forsaken place. Well, I s'pose it was best to go to her husband but, what a life, with three children. Well, I'm glad I'm single after that, and if my husband can't keep me comfortably, one child will be enough. Mightn't be able to get even that, so it's no good talking is it? I have sent in Andy's *(her brother, Andrew Richard Avenell, born in 1888 The Two Mile, Queensland)* name to the base to find out if he has arrived. They take two months to come over these days.

The food question is starting in the papers these days. Not that it seems necessary to live on black bread, but when you know the Savoy, Ritz and big cafes have twenty-four different soups, fourteen different fishes to choose from, it's absurd. The poor people will be starving later. Lloyd George is taking control of the food.

Referendum was very funny in Australia, eh. What a lot of the Irish are staying at home. All to do with home rule. Fancy, Mr Ashton not enlisting, no people, no ties. I had some "Mercurys" *(newspapers)* from Bert Norris the other day and saw his name. Fancy, the Boltons going bung, even Mrs B's wedding presents were sold and I always thought they were rolling in money, didn't you, racey etc. Silly man. And of course, I read of the Town Clerk, really everything seems to be the same.

(section missing) ... and I went to "Daddy Long Legs", Oh, it was pretty. The beginning was a scene from an asylum *(orphanage)* with a visit from the Trustees showing up some very dirty doings and the finish Judy is sent and educated at College, it was awfully pretty.

I think I've seen all the theatres now except Mr Wu, it's supposed to be good. Colonel Dawson and Captain Crane took the three of us. We met them on furlough. I had a very busy day and it is bitterly cold. I saw snow yesterday for the first time, it was very small flakes and only a little like sugar crystals. Quite a number of us haven't seen snow, so you can guess there was some excitement and amusement to the English maids we have. We have just received a challenge: Sister, who is in my ward, against forty-two one-armed boys. They are waiting for their limbs from America, and we are going to have a snowball fight. Len and Bob (*Queenie's young brothers*) would love to be in, I know.

I expect I shall see a great change in them on my return home. They will be young men. I sent them a book each and am cabling five pounds home, Mum, to you all for Christmas. I haven't got much money these days. I have had to buy such a lot of warm clothes. One of the sisters took your blouses. Hope Doll's won't be too big, but they are good and cool. I must send Jim something, some nice cool socks, I think, when next I go to town. It is such a bustle, but if you only saw me getting all over London on my own. Piccadilly to the Strand is no distance and Westminster. I soon got my bearings and you can't get there on foot because you don't know the way; hop in the tube and you're there.

I had a nice letter from Bill Cowton last week. He hopes to be over here soon on leave so I will see him, although they are in action now on the Somme and he might get a "Blighty-knock". Have not heard from Jack Earwaker for some weeks or Tom Cole either. I've written to the base about them. Have not heard of Billie Lee. *(He was at Aldershot Officers School at the time).* Rollie is back in action some time now. They will be lucky if they get out of it all safely.

Well, Mum I wrote you a few weeks ago. Aunty writes to me and Charlie Palmer *(the step-son of Emily Palmer, Ilford. Emily was previously married to Queenie's uncle George Avenell)* wrote me from Ireland where he is in hospital from France. Aunty wants me to meet him (don't know why)? I am wearing clothes and clothes and still I shiver. Poor old Doll. I wrote to her at Innisfail. Tell her to cheer up and not to worry, she's too young to do that yet. Hope you have all had a nice Christmas when this reaches you. Tons of love dearest Mum and boys. I wish I was home, we are all very homesick.

I shall come back as soon as I can. Much love,

xxxx Queenie xxxxx

Prosthesis Workshop, Southall London, Australian Auxiliary Hospital. (AWM D00544)

The artificial limbs, Southall London, Australian Auxiliary Hospital. (AWM D00550)

Australian Military Hospital, Southall,
30th November, 1916.

Dearest Mum, Doll and boys,

I am on night duty and having a very busy time. In surgical wards, all very special operations, such as removal of bulbous nerves from stumps, artificial wrists etc. That is most interesting when a boy has only his hand taken off. The doctors can now operate on the wrist and cut the bone in half making a joint. Of course, the skin has to be cut to get at the bone, but it heals up and yet the bone is separate, then he can use the hand, etc. They are going back to Australia and are all just shattered wrecks, really. I am sorry for Australia, for it will be nothing but broken down men after the war.

By the way, a rumour has it that Germany has sent her first request for peace. Two Zeppelins were brought down in the north and Taubes actually came over London. It was very foggy so the aircraft were not much good. Things are not too bright on the other side, and war is still on. Not that you would notice in Piccadilly Circus. I loathe this night work, as you know, but still I haven't been on since I first was in France, so I can't growl and I've only got a month. I might be off for Christmas.

I wonder how you all are and poor old Dolly and Bob. My word, Mum it will be a relief to get out of the army and I hope we shall have six months together just living a quiet life and good chums. I won't know Bob and Len, they will be growing so much and Jim is still sprouting too. I've just received a draught *(money order)* from Coley – five pounds for Tom, and I can't get any news of him lately, have not heard from Jack Earwaker either, so I s'pose they're gone like many others, only I wouldn't say anything to Coley yet. I am making enquiries at the base about him and they have such numbers of casualties they are upside down. However, I have wired to his O.C. about him in France.

Bert Norris was up again last week and today he writes saying they are off to France, poor devil. I hope he has good luck. Had a letter from Auntie, saying she had heard from you. It is ages since I had a letter. I'm sorry now I didn't cable, but I thought you might get upset and wonder why I was in England, so it's better to get a letter. Charlie Palmer wrote to me from Ireland where he is stationed. He's a Lieutenant. I shall send you on their letters.

Oh, I can't get any news of Andy, of course, he may not have arrived yet. Uncle is looking out for him too. I can't think what has become of him. He knows where to find me. All the sisters know me and besides No. 1 A.G.H. always send my letters here to me. I s'pose you know I am in England by now and can go all over London by myself. It's great fun getting lost down the tubes. What a talk we shall have Mum, together. I want to go out to Windsor Castle as soon as I can. Oh, but this night duty – you know I can't stand any nervy work.

All my boys are either winged or legs off, shoulders blown away, big head wounds, but nearly all healed up and just little pieces of dead bone keeping them from healing up altogether. They are such fine fellows. Some have ONLY had 12 operations. I believe the new limbs are just wonderful, one boy was given his legs (both artificial), free, as an ad by the (American contractor) firm, and he can go upstairs, walked seven miles route march without any sticks or crutches, so if he can do that with two artificial limbs, a one-legged man can be almost normal. It's good too, for they are helpless wretches and would give you the nightmare.

I have just bought a new coat and skirt, grey uniform, Norfolk Style, it is our new uniform, really. I have a grey flannel tweed, straps and stars up of course. Saw the first fall of snow the other day. Bert said they had quite a heavy one down at Salisbury Plain and some of the men made great snow men. Lasted two days.

Well, Mum it is awfully cold and dreary weather. I haven't seen the sun for weeks and I don't s'pose we will for months. Sunny Queensland, eh? Oh my! These grey days of England. Am sending you a bundle of papers to read.

Much love to you all and a Happy New Year.

xxxxx Queenie.

Chapter 9: England, 1917

Australian Military Hospital, Southall,
6th January, 1917.

Dearest Mum and all at home,

It is a fortnight since I last wrote. I am off night duty at last after six weeks, making five months this year, so I think that alone is enough to send anyone dippy for a while. However, day duty is very nice after it, especially a decent sleep at night. I do not feel like writing somehow. Poor old Coley, I don't know what she must think of me.

I received seven registered letters from Mrs Markwell, Earwaker and Bond with money for the grandsons, which I have delivered "toute suite", so I hope the poor old boys have got it alright. It came on Christmas Eve, and since then another for myself from Mrs Earwaker with a one pound note. They are awfully good really. Coley sent me one pound for Christmas. It was very useful. For three pounds per fortnight is hard to live on and boots, etc, are so dear. I manage quite as well as the sisters that draw their full pay and always look better in my clothes; I don't mean in looks, but my uniform. Laundry is very expensive; in fact, everything is.

Peace talk has all dropped and seems to be nothing doing. They seem to have great hopes for the signing. In the London papers it says Queensland is in flood and Rockhampton in great danger of being swept away and sixty people drowned in Clermont. It is awful. The war is quite enough these days and they can't blame the Germans, can they? *(Grandma Avenell's note: I think she means for the floods.)*

I went to a theatre "Romance", the first night I came off *(night duty)*. A "wingy" officer took me. Poor devil's lost his right arm and was great Sydney athlete. Oh, but "Romance" was gorgeous. Really, Doris Keans was very clever and took the part of Madam Cavalini an Italian Opera singer, who falls in love with a clergyman, rector of St. Giles. She speaks broken English, of course, but very clever. I went one afternoon to "Flying Colours", a revue, but it is nothing like "Romance". I have been wanting to see it for some time.

Do you remember Dudley Salmon of the Lascelles' Station? *(Cattle station in North Queensland)* I met him in town one day. He is an officer, but is going into the Flying Corps. Eve Lascelles is a flying man too, but has been very badly wounded. Of course, he still flies, but not in France. I think I have a pal of Bill Cowton in my ward, a chap named Oliver from the School of Mines, Charters

Towers. I can't get any information of Andy, but headquarters have promised to let me know.

Billie Lee is over and coming to see me, so a sister he met tells me. He is looking very well. Had a letter from Bert Norris, he says his luck was in, for he was sent a mile back from the front line on Christmas Day to make duck boards, in charge of a fatigue party, so they enjoyed their dinner, in peace, if not quite out of danger. I can't get any trace of Tom Cole. He does not write and I send him letters, papers, parcels and now this money. I have made all sorts of inquiries; he wrote last from a New Zealand hospital with a septic poisoning of some sort. Jack Earwaker writes me little notes, but Cyril Chambers, I have not heard from him.

I am now in a Ward D and E, mostly stumps (legs) either being re-amputated bulbous nerves, muscles, etc., they give me such hurry-ups sometimes. One "ammoned" *(pretended)* to faint just now with his wooden leg on. You can hardly tell them, really, when they get used to them. They have a big recreation room just under our ward and a concert is on now. The people give heaps of concerts and parties, etc. Twenty of our boys went out to some big knobs at South Kensington, an "At Home" just for the boys. They got a music party and thoroughly enjoyed themselves.

I have not heard from you, but received my dear little Christmas gifts and thanks so much, they were so useful. I made the tea on a special day in my room and my powder puff was very grubby. I got some awfully nice presents from some of the girls. I only bought a half dozen hanks *(handkerchiefs)*, and gave my own pals one each, but I got a sweet boudoir cap and creton box *(sic)* and huge box of chocs from a wingy officer, one dozen hanks, a cigarette box, a pretty scented sachet of lavender, serviette ring, so it was not so depressing to know that you are not forgotten, and your parcel came just before Christmas. I was on night duty but got up. Most of the patients went out after dinner to friends, those that could hobble.

I must try and get down to Auntie's next week some time but I work jolly hard all day and my afternoon off I'm glad to go to bed. It's been glorious weather for England, quite mild for this time of the year, but today it's started off again and a real freezer. I do wish we could all go home. It's funny, Mum, how I get round London tubes, underground, buses and trains, you can't go wrong, and when once you know where Oxford Circus, Piccadilly Circus, Trafalgar Square is, you are right. Then, our A.I.F. Headquarters is in Victoria, so we go there often.

Well, dearest Mum, and all, I'll say au revoir, till next week. Much love and kisses to you all, Doll and Ken and Babies. I wonder if Doll is up in Innisfail yet. I hope to hear from you all soon.

xxxx Queenie.

Australian Military Hospital, Southall,
18th January, 1917.

Dearest Mum and all at home,

Andy has arrived at last. I had a parcel all ready for him. Flannel pyjamas, gloves, cigs, tobacco, pipe, soap, Bovril, handkerchiefs. I only bought the gloves, the rest were "backsheesh" (presents). I have another pair of pyjamas. I wore them in France in the cold tents, but now I wear nighties, and a fire in my room. Comfort!

I heard that there wasn't a blanket to give the troops that arrived with Andy. The first night, 12,000 too, so they must have shivered in the cold. It was snowing and about a foot deep. I'll be glad when the cold weather is over, only another two months. I think then I shall be sent back to France. I do not mind at all, for I feel well enough and the girls are all breaking down over there and must be relieved.

I expect Andy up here any day on four days leave. Shall see him also about your allowance. Have quite a lot to talk to him about. We can go down to Auntie's together. I have not been for some time. They had a terrible time coming over, but I expect Andy has told you all about it. Bill Cowton has been over on leave. We went to a theatre together. Grand opera, "Aida", a beautiful Egyptian tale, but I'm not very keen on that sort of thing, yelling and screaming at one another.

I'm going to "Romance" again tomorrow, I told you about it didn't I? Doris Keane is glorious and I'm going to "The Misleading Lady" at night. I like a matinee best because I can't stand the late hour at night and on duty next day, but I've got a friend over from the front and he wants to see these plays and won't go alone. Begged me to go with him so I've got to help them that way. Men hate going to theatres alone. I had dinner last night at the Piccadilly hotel. Tomorrow a table is booked at the Savoy. I go in my uniform always, which is rather smart looking now. A grey coat and skirt and Norfolk coat. I will get Andy to have his photo taken with me just for you.

We are getting more stumps every day and have now about 300 without legs and arms. Yesterday a crowd of the boys were out having a snow fight. Crutches everywhere in the snow and only their one leg. I have about thirty leg stumps to dress every morning and about forty beds to make. The orderly helps me. It is an awful rush and I wonder whether I'm on my head or heels. One thing the time just flies and before I know its dinner time. All the time they are joking with one another and are very happy. My wingy officer friend has gone from here to Roehampton getting his artificial arm. Poor old chap, he is then going on to train the men at Salisbury Plains and refuses to be discharged. I quite agree with him. No one-eyed soldier is being sent home now. They are going back to the front.

It will be a mighty big push in the spring alright, I'm sure. The Germans are getting their wind up and very scared. It will be great living at home in Australia once again.

Well, Mum you will get letters from Andy now. If Jim is not coming away, I hope he gets a transfer south, not Brisbane tho' it's a dusty deadly place. Hope you got the five pounds I cabled. Much love to you all.

Xxxxxxx Queenie

P.S. Jack Earwaker is over here and coming to me this week.

Snowfight at Southall, with Queenie pictured with some of her patients.

Australian Military Hospital, Southall,
28th January, 1917.

Dearest Mum, Doll and Boys,

Just received your two letters. Its nice to hear of Dollie's return to Innisfail, because I know if Mrs Cole is near her, she will be well looked after. Have had a long letter from her too, telling me all about Dolly being there. You must be relieved to know at last they have a home. And my cook Bella Stewart, (Bob knows her), looked after the baby, while Doll did her shopping. Well, it's funny how things turn round. They are such gossipy lot of people in country towns as a rule, but the Innisfail people did really treat me well. Of course, I was there only seven months.

I'm sitting on the floor on my rug near the fire waiting for Andy. He is coming up to London on four days leave. It's my afternoon off but I don't think I can go out because I've got a fearful cold and throat. It's bitterly cold just now. Ice everywhere. He says he has a cold too, so I might make him stay in hospital for a few days. Everybody has colds. Auntie says it's the coldest winter she has known for years. So we are really standing it well so far.

Two of the sisters fainted yesterday and one today. They are run down and the cold affects the poor circulation, I s'pose. I trot out most of my off-duty time and I think it does me more good than sitting over a fire in my room. Bill Cowton has been over, he stayed with Mr Callendar's people in Sussex and we had a day in London together. He has got very thin. Poor beggars, those trenches this weather. I guess they live on rum.

29th: Well, Mum, Andy arrived and two pals with him. They were hungry, nothing to eat from Salisbury, so while they went out to the "Red Lion" next door for something to eat, I made a bright fire in our little sitting room and we sat there till 6 p.m. I could hardly speak, but my cold is better today. Well, I had a place for them to stay, "Peel House" Overseas club in Victoria Street, just near our base, Horseferry Road, and we are going to meet tomorrow outside the Army and Navy Stores and go down to see Auntie at Ilford. I've just sent her a wire that we are coming.

One of our nurses is to be married in the morning from here and Matron is giving her a morning breakfast tea. All the boys are standing with an archway of crutches on their one leg. If you like, I will write a full account of it. Andy was well, not much of a cold but very thin, no wonder, they had very little to eat on the boat coming over, ran out of everything as it was such a long journey. My old boat, you know, that I came home on, an awful tub too. Well, I hope we have a good day tomorrow.

So strange I've just received another letter from you with one for Andy enclosed so it came quickly considering dated 8th December. I told them to go to "Peg O My Heart" last night, "Chu Chin Chow" (with Oscar Asche) tonight. You see it's my long day on today. Tomorrow I might go to something with Andy, but my cold is nearly better. I don't like staying out at night, it means 12.30 in bed and up on a long day. I like matinees myself. Its fine, the same as night as it's quite dark at 4 p.m. although now the evenings are getting longer. Summer in England will be nice, I hope I won't have to go to France yet awhile.

Andy thinks they will train in a base in France. We have not had a decent talk yet, but tomorrow we will be by ourselves. They tubed from Waterloo to Paddington Street on their own, not bad, but I'm glad we are together here. I thought you would be glad to know I was in London for some time. Poor old Doll, I feel very much relieved to hear of your circumstances being much brighter. It's a pity Jim is not transferred tho' his commercial city experience would help him later with his own bank. Hope Len has been successful *(in the Queensland scholarship exam)*.

I told Andy to go to the Tower today. It's such an education all these sights, even Madame Tussauds, with all the present and ancient celebrities and the Monarchs. I wonder you never went there. Really of course, the horrors, I hate that sort of thing. I would like to have taken all boys to a good café for the music and tea. I might leave Auntie's early tomorrow yet; the Trocadero is quite a swanky place, and a good programme on from 4 p.m. till 6 p.m. and tea for one and six. Soldiers' price compared to ordinary price – anything to 10 shillings. The Savoy, Carlton and Ritz are just the same.

Mother, I screamed to myself the other day – I went out with an officer, a friend of mine in Egypt. He has lost his right leg and got the Military Cross. It was his first furlough with his new limb. Well, we dined at the Savoy, had a box at the Gaiety for "Theodore and Co." – it only cost four pounds, fifteen shillings, the box I mean. The dinner was the usual fizz, of course, but imagine me swanking round like that and coming from Innisfail, Queensland, walking into Parry's shop for a sixpence ice. Oh dear, its great fun, you know while I'm in England. My turn soon for France.

Well, I asked Andy how much he had, he said a fiver so I thought they had better stay at the Overseas Club. One and six a room, bath and breakfast. Go out anywhere, you get own meals. They only draw one shilling a day, so we laughed. They will have a good time. Andy says he writes you all his experiences, so you will have a really good budget from us both. I am going to get him to come with me for our photo tomorrow together for you, if possible. I shall write you again in a few days tell you all about the wedding tomorrow. She's got a Colonel and he just got a D.S.O. What ho!! Haven't seen the Colonel yet, but it will be very interesting, I think, all in uniform.

Well, I must go to sleep. Sorry you have not received your little brooch. I will get you another and give it to a Sister. Have you got the blouses yet? Dolly will be glad of hers at Innisfail. I will send her a pretty little frock next time I go to town, they are so cheap in the white sales now. I want a set of furs badly but can't afford them. We are not allowed to wear them of course. All uniform.

Heaps of love dearest mum, and kidlets.

Queenie.

P.S. Don't worry about us, I am alright.

No. 2 Australian Military Hospital, Southall,
9th February, 1917.

Dearest Mum, Doll and the boys,

I seem to be getting a letter from you two and three times a week lately, so I send them all on to Andy. Also, Dollie's letter was very cheerful and if I don't feel too tired I will drop her a line. Well, Andy has changed his camp again and is now at No. 10 Camp Dorrington, Salisbury Plains. They have transferred all the T.M.B.s (Trench Mortar Battalions) into the infantry, much to their disgust, but I am going to try to get Andy into the school for officers. I don't see why he shouldn't; he would get much more money and comforts. He was not thinking about it until I suggested it, so now he is quite keen. I have already spoken to an officer friend of mine and he is going to see about it. But, I think he has to go to France first. However, I'll let you know later.

Well, Mum this is a cold rotten country. I shiver and shiver. It's all snow outside, ice, wet and slippery. I was awfully glad to get your cable three days after you sent it, so that's jolly quick, isn't it? So Len has passed. I bought a great book the other day for him for four and six. I want to send Jim some cigs and a cig case. I hope Bob and Len have received their books for Christmas. Your letters are coming direct to me now.

I have Jack Earwaker in my ward. His feet are improving but he can't walk very well yet. Geoffrey Greer of Innisfail is in my ward too. He has only one leg though and is such a bonnie young fellow. They are all splendid. They keep so bright. There are several different makes of artificial limbs. The Rowley, Ernst, and Essential, etc., etc., and they have such arguments which is the best.

I was wondering, Mother, if you could do anything for my other star. I am only one of a hundred staff nurses, of course, but still why shouldn't we get promotion as well as others, and we have tried over here, but it can only be done from Australia. On May 15, I shall be two years in the army. You see, I am only a staff nurse. There have not been any promotions since the first "Kyarra" went over to Egypt. (Sister Echlin's lot). She was only a staff nurse but after twelve months service they all applied and got made a Sister and now they have two stars.

I think if you wrote to that man who used to know us years ago. He is the top dog over the Minister for Defence, his name is Dodds, and explain that I have been in the service two years and of course, Mum, be careful what you say. I might have to put a proper application in still. There's nothing like trying and I don't care if they give me the dirty throw out. It means more money, too.

Glad Thomas is on transport duty and leaves tomorrow for Australia. She sent her "best wishes to you". I don't envy her the risk. The ships that are sunk in the last few days are awful. America is still dallying and the longer she keeps out the better for us, isn't it? Haven't much more news. I told you about Andy and I going down to Auntie's for the day. She had a nice lunch and was so glad to have us. She is very jolly and feels lonely when all the boys are at the war.

Must ring off now, much love and kisses to you all.

Queenie.

P.S. Of course, Mum, if you don't think it wise about the appointment for a Sister, it doesn't matter, but in the British Army all the sisters get their promotion after a year's service. In the A.I.F. so far they don't. Love to you all. Queenie.

No. 2 Australian Auxiliary Hospital, Southall,
17th February, 1917.

Dearest Mum and all at home,

I don't feel in a very good mood to write letters, the weather is horrid and seems to have such a dopey, fatiguing effect on one. It's all grey days, snow has gone for a while. It rained this morning a bit, the sun came out for a few minutes and now it's foggy. I'm off duty, but my room is over a fire feeling fed up with things in general. The piece of good news I have: Andy went into the Officer's School three days ago, so that will be promotion, a Second Lieutenant. He blossoms out. I have to finance him for his mess. It's one and six a day, so I can do that.

I must try and save after this. I never have a stiver and I want to go to Scotland on my next leave. Can't do it for less than ten pounds. I get a free pass, of course. I gave Andy two pounds while he was on leave and so I'm jolly glad he will have his commission as he can look after me instead. Eighteen shillings a day will be his allowance. He can get this alright and has brains as good as many I know.

Poor Len, passing his exams. I don't know if it's a scholarship for the Jervis Bay College. I hope it's the latter, myself. I know how keen he is on the Navy. Andy feels the difference already. An officer has so many more privileges; I expect he will go to France almost at once when he's through. I may be going back there any day, too. They want as many as they can get for the Spring. I really don't feel fit for it, but I will do my best. I feel weary and worn out now. It's the climate that's so trying.

I have Jack Earwaker in my ward still. He is nearly alright but very run down after ten months in the trenches. It is only to be expected. Well, now isn't it strange – while he was here we saw in the paper where Cyril Chambers had shot himself at the hotel in London. We all made enquiries and it was Jack Earwaker's own cousin. Of course, he had been buried three days when we found out, so were very upset. He had only written to me a fortnight before saying he would come and see Jack and me. He was only twenty-five years and had got his commission and the M.C. *(Military Cross).* His poor mother will be terribly upset. I have written to her and Mrs Earwaker.

I don't get the time to write much and I think I want a long rest and at times feel like asking for transport, only I'm scared of torpedoes. England seems to be confident the war will be over the end of this year. I hope so, and we shall be together once again. I wish you could get away from Queensland. The last letter I wrote I told you about the Sisterships. I don't know if you can do anything for me to get my promotion. It seems so absurd; it has to come from Australia. It is a rather delicate thing, they recall us on the least thing; tell you they don't require your services any longer. Still, I don't think they would mind a staff nurse asking for her promotion and influence seems to be the only thing these days.

I have chilblains on my feet and oh, they are awful. I'm in a real grumpy mood, aren't I? But it's not very bright and cheerful in this hospital; the number of boys with their legs missing is dreadful. Hope to hear from you soon. It's nearly a fortnight since your last letter arrived. I send all letters down to Andy.

Much love to you all dears.

xxxxxx Queenie.

Editor's note: Southall Australian Auxiliary hospital, (previously the Otto Monsted Hospital, originally the Margarine Factory recreation building). The hospital became a Military Hospital in 1915 and treated 3,300 soldiers during the war, losing only four in their care. In an era before antibiotics, this is an incredible tribute to the doctors and nurses especially when you consider the terrible amputations most suffered. Details from Dr. Jonathon Oates history of Southall).

Letter to Queenie's younger brother, Len:

Southall,
29th February, 1917,

My dear little brother,

This is just a few lines all to yourself to congratulate you on your exam and also thanks for such a delightful letter received yesterday. I read it out to the one-legged boys (dinkum kangaroos) and we thoroughly enjoyed the news from dear old Australia. I sent you a good book with a p.c. of some of the boys in my ward.

Well, by now of course, you know Andy is getting his commission and will be a Lieutenant.

Len Avenell, Queenie's youngest brother, Townsville, 1914, aged 10.

I am going down to Tidworth to see him on Saturday, so will be away all day. It only takes two hours to get there, and costs twelve and threepence with a warrant from headquarters. Am glad you have received the books. Mum said you had read them twice. I never forgot how keen you are on reading, especially modern literature, which is mostly war. (Zeppelins, Naval, and trenches).

I must see what I can get you at Harrods to help with your division. I can drive a car myself now and hold a chaffeuse certificate. Well, this is writing under difficulties so I must "finie". We are giving Matron an afternoon tea at the Elysee in honour of her R.R.C. *(Royal Red Cross Medal)*. Will send you a B. Australasian later.

Write again, my dear little brother. I'm awfully glad to hear you are so clever. If you cannot get a Jervis Bay scholarship, try and be a Doctor. I would rather you were in the Navy though, it is a grand life.

Much love,

xxxxxxx Queenie.

No. 2 Australian Auxiliary Hospital, Southall,
8th March, 1917.

Dearest Mum and all at home,

It's a bitter cold windy day. I can't get warm sitting over a fire even and March in Townsville is as hot as Hades, so there you are. Next month, of course, the weather will be better, but it has been a bitter winter. Well, I had a day at Peckam Downs last week with Andy. He cannot get his commission till he is in the trenches three weeks. So he will only be another month at Candaha Barracks.

I had dinner at an adjoining camp with Mr Shamallick and Lieutenant Trundle of Brisbane (Auntie Jessie's friends). And the O.C. motored me to Andover where I caught a train for Waterloo, then I tubed to Paddington (15 min) and then the train again for Southall, so you can guess the busy day I had, and I was tired. The country air was great and I feel such a lot better too. We went for a bonnie walk over Tidworth in the afternoon. At dinner, the O.C. toasted the first Australian Sister they had had with them. They want me to come down again. I might, near the end of Andy's course.

Len, I s'pose is going to the Grammar by now. I hope he will study hard for the Jervis Bay College, then we can all live in Sydney. I can hardly hold this pen, it's so darned cold. George Cole has arrived. He wrote me a letter and I've had a long letter from Tom, which I sent on to Coley. Poor Cyril Chambers! I only wish he were well and alive too. I s'pose Bob will want to come over and fight too. And we will be lucky if we get home alright. Great success on the Tigris, but in France they are now beginning the supposed grand finale. I can see us all here in three year's time.

I have not been to any theatres lately, so can't tell you about the new shows. I hear they are all very tropical. Hope we shall all be home soon. Received papers about the Clermont flood, it's all too dreadful and realize I can't think of it, the poor things, it was worse than being bombed out.

Much love to you and Doll and Ken, and the babies, from

Queenie.

Southall,
18th March, 1917.

Dearest Mum and all at home,

I do not feel in a very good letter writing mood tonight, but I'm afraid it's over my usual weekly letter and you will wonder what's up. I heard from Andy yesterday, he is alright and still going on at the school. He will only be there about another week and then will be sent off to the front where he gets his commission. I hope he will be lucky and dodge Fritz.

Isn't the news awfully good and by the time this reaches you it will be better still I hope. We are nearing the end. Poor old Kitchener, not to see it, though the Dardanelles report seems to be giving him a lot of the blame, but only for him, where would we have been at the outbreak of war? I've just had a letter from Tom and George Cole, they are both well. George expects to be coming up to London on his four days leave, so I will see him and take him down to his Aunt Lou's. She is a sweet old lady with such pretty girls, and also very capable too. One is a private secretary to a Solicitor, fancy.

Had a long letter from Bert Norris yesterday. He is right in the middle of it all, of course. Tommie Lloyd of Mackay is just near here and called to see me the other day. I was out, oh and at the Colliseum saw "Mad Genie", with Vesta Tilley, I s'pose you saw the latter when a girl, as I believe she is 65. To look at her on the stage she is about seventeen years. Impersonates a man and does a turn, "Six days leave". She is simply ripping and sings "The Next Time They Give Me Six Day's Leave, I'd Rather Have Six Months Hard" and then she sings another song about a boy who has a fortnight's holiday every year, and she says "It's Woodbines I Fear For The Rest Of The Year". Till next July. "Genie" was splendid too. In between the acts, Frank Lester (was one of the Bing Boys when on), auctioneered a box and got 35 guineas for it. A matinee next week in aid of Sisters.

Well, I'm glad to hear Doll and Ken are getting on in Innisfail. I'm saving up my small cash now for a trip to Scotland. We get a free railway pass and my next leave is due in a month's time so I hope I can go. Leave is stopped in France, don't know if it will be here. I have not been sent back to France, yet. Still I did seven months there and deserve at least six months over here. I hope we get your letter this week. Another Zeppelin was brought down in France. It is a loss of a quarter of a million pounds to the Germans to bring a Zep down, so as it did not do any damage, they are having a general knockback all round. I will hurry up to bed now and write again to Jim in a few days. Much love to you all.

xxxxxx Queenie.

P.S. I do wish Jim had a transfer south before we get home. Q

Southall,
25th March, 1917.

Dearest Mum and all at home,

I wonder what you are thinking of the latest events. Sometimes we think the war will end in a few months and then just the opposite. However, we have been giving the Huns a few knocks, still its going to take some push shortly. We are all in a state of not exactly excitement, but knowing this big battle is being prepared for by both sides, we wonder what will happen.

I went down to the camp yesterday to see Andy and he thought he would surprise me and came up so we missed each other. It was a shame, because he may be off to France any day in time for the big battle. I met Raymond Croker on my way home. He is up in Grantham training with the Lewis Guns. We had a great old yarn.

I also met Captain Kelsea down at an Officer's Hospital at Cobham in Kent. Isn't it funny how we meet in England? Met Tom Jack yesterday too, and going into town the other day, one of our M.O.S. got into my carriage and it was a Captain Nisbett from Townsville and had stitched up Bole's cut. He got married at Salisbury and his wife is coming here to live (a Sydney girl). He seems a very nice young fellow, and we had a great old talk of Townsville.

I told you about George Cole arriving. Well on Friday last I went down to Mrs Gyles and saw him. I'm sure Coley will be delighted to know George has been up and is quite well but for an old cough and cold, which seems to be quite the usual thing for all Australians to have. One minute it is snowing and blowing hard, and the next the sun is out. Such peculiar weather. I'm quite satisfied Aussie will be good enough for me. Have not seen Auntie lately, but I will run down some time shortly.

Have not been to any theatres lately, not since the Colliseum last week, I told you about. Oh, I heard today you are not getting many of our letters, quite a number of boats with our mail have been torpedoed. I have not received a letter from you for three weeks and only one last mail. I'm sure you write more than two letters in six weeks, don't you?

Well, Mum dear, we will have such a lot to talk about. I wish we were coming home soon. I'm terribly tired of it all. It's no use thou'.

Much love to you all and xxxxx Queenie.

P.S. Tell Dolly to tell Mrs Calendar I was with a Lieut. Andrews yesterday, his son is in the artillery, his wife in a canteen over here and his daughter in a munitions factory and he himself has had a crack on the head, been trephaned but still carrying on with Home Service. Fancy the whole family out in it.

Note: on back of page from Grandma Avenell to Mrs Cole, Innisfail: 'Coley dear, Latest from Q. Will write myself next week. Very seedy Rheaums: and a big boil on temple. Run down, eh!

31st May, 1917.'

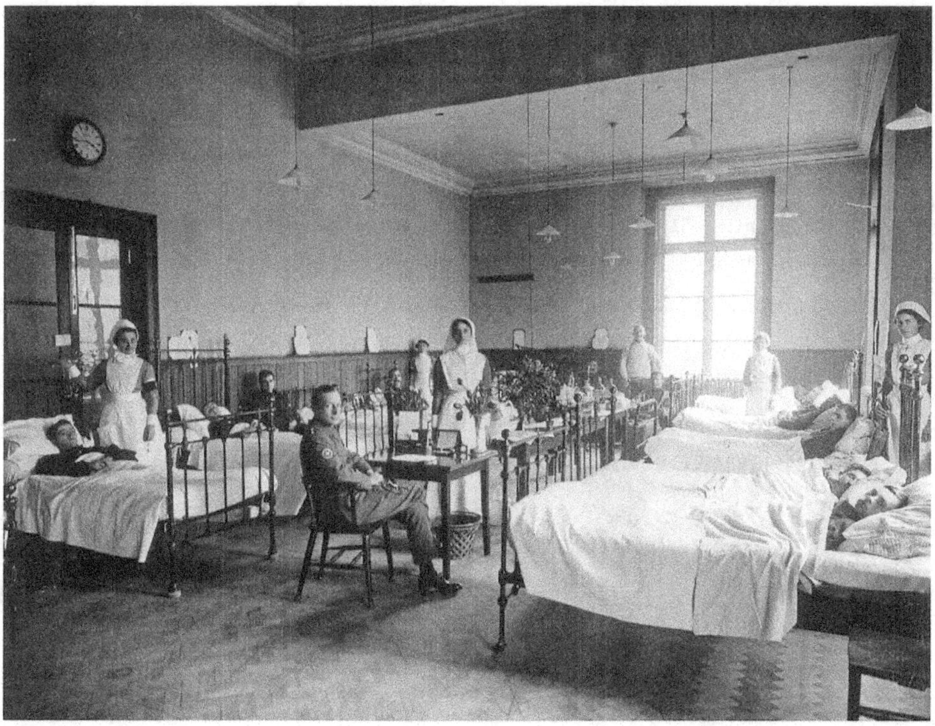

A ward in the Australian Auxiliary Hospital, Southall, during the First World War.

No. 2 Australian Auxiliary Hospital, Southall,
1st April, 1917.

Dearest Mum and boys and Doll,

Just received a letter from Coley where she has noticed Len's pass in the paper. I s'pose you were all very excited. I hope he will have a good holiday and rest for a while, then go at his exams hard, for the quicker he goes into the Jervis Bay College, really the better for him. *(Note ed. Poor Dad never got into the Navy, no money, and was at work by 15).* Tell him, Hugh Black came out to see me yesterday, he is in the Artillery School for Officers and has grown and filled tremendously.

I can't help wishing Jim would enlist and come anyway, as you, Mum, would still have fifteen pounds and eight shillings a month. It is only the right thing to do and any man that does not do his bit, isn't worth much. A little boy in my ward with his leg off and just turned 17 years after a year's fighting. He feels far happier than the man that has two legs and stops at home. I shall write to Jim, myself. It means every man.

Well enough of this. News is much the same. I don't think it's a week since I wrote. I had my birthday and never remembered till it was nearly over, so that's active service, eh what. Andy evidently did not remember it either. He is still waiting to return to France. I don't think he can get his commission till he's been in the trenches and quite right too, isn't it? The weather is awful – snow, slush, sleet and mud. Still I go about in it. Sent your letter down to Andy, it was dated the 4th of January and three weeks ago your letters received dated 25th January, so one must have come via the Cape. Have had letters from Bill Cowton and Bert Norris. They are all well, but a friend of mine Trevor Francis, Captain and M.C. has been killed, this last week.

Well, Mum, I tell you every letter we're fed up with the blooming war. Mrs Gyles, Mr Cole's sister, is so kind and sweet. George stayed with them while on leave. Isn't it funny me meeting these people? I sometimes wonder shall we ever get home again. The food is the burning question or topic. We are going without tea between meals and just having the three meals a day. It's quite enough too.

I sent Bill Cowton a parcel the other day, but can't afford to very often. I hear Vivian Bernard is a prisoner of war in Germany. What a pity, for they are being starved. I must try and get a parcel sent over to him if I can. I feel my share of work is so little and yet we can't do more. My turn in France will about settle me to want to do more. The sun is just peeping out and everywhere is snow, it's a beautiful picture. Till next week, much love to you all and a big hug.

Queenie.

P.S. Was very amused at Len's letter and well, still, the change ought to do him good. Glad to hear you are going to have a holiday at a hotel for Easter. Will think of you all next week. Q.

Easter – Western Fever Hospital, Homerton, N.E.
12th April, 1917.

Dearest Mum and boys,

I got the German measles last Thursday and bundled off here "Toute suite". That accounts for the new address. I hope to return to Southall on Saturday. Have not been very ill, more like a bad cold, sniffly and sneezy, but the rash was very thick. I feel better then, but have to be isolated a week to keep from the other sisters and patients. Jolly miserable being shut up in a room alone and the food is anything but good. However I shall be back soon at Southall. The sisters have been very good and written to me.

I had a letter card from Andy. He does not know I'm in here, but I've written and sent him your letters which came from Auntie dated the 20th January, 1917. I got them yesterday and poor old Grandad's letter about Billie Lee, *(Her cousin, Major H. W. Lee, 'Willie' aged 24),* and I'm very much afraid he is among the list killed. I've written to Reg Sellars, who is in the 4th Pioneers to ask him about it. There might be another Major H.W. Lee, of course, but I suppose it's only too true. I hear Clive *(Willie's much younger brother)* was coming out too. I s'pose you get all the little bits of news every day.

I see by yesterday's paper, our hero, Robinson V.C., who brought down the first Zeppelin at Aiffly, is missing and believed killed in that air raid they made the other day. It's all too sad. Well, Mum, I keep thinking Jim must come away. Can't he leave the Union Bank under the arrangements, he can go back "après le guerre"? I have just received a letter from a little Mackay boy. I don't know him, but perhaps Jim does. He wants me to go to see him and I will when I get out of here. If they give me any leave, I am going to either Scotland or Killarney. I may not get any, still I'll have a try, as it's seven months since I had a fortnight's holiday, so my next letter will be either from three places, Scotland, Ireland or Southall!!!

The night before I got sick, I went to see Gaby Deslys in "Suey Susette"; she is just glorious. I went with Hugh Black, who is at Lord's training for an officer in the Artillery. We just loved it. Her dresses were absolutely superb. Next to the "Chu Chin Chow" and "The Maid Of The Mountains", it is the best. I often think of you all and wish you could be with me when I'm flying round. In the afternoon we motored through Hyde Park and round down the embankment just to put in time before having dinner, and you know the taxi only registered five and twopence *(52 cents)* for nearly an hour, so it's really not dear. I hear "Romance" and "Peg O' My Heart" is playing in Melbourne and Sydney now. They will love them both. I'm sure I wrote you between those dates in November, it was while I was on leave and I used to scribble you a few pages at the Windsor, I told you all about the Lord Mayor's show, etc., St Paul's, Westminster Abbey, etc.

I often see our boys in their khaki and slouch hats stand gazing at Nelson's Monument in the Square. It appeals to them more than anything. I can hear an aeroplane overhead just now. Its burr is quite loud and yet they are well up in the air. What a marvellous air raid that was on the German lines, did you read *(about)* it? Fifty of our ships went up, dropped bombs and fired machine guns on the front lines and then in the middle, fifty German ships came up and tackled them. Of course, then our troops went over and took the trenches, but our machines had a tussle to get back. I read a wonderful description of it by a wounded flying officer. Will get it and send it to you if I can.

Well, I have no special news. Auntie wrote to me but did not know I was in here of course. Charlie Palmer is coming home for a week. He's been sick. Fancy Mrs Rhodes taking in boarders, rather funny, isn't it? Money grabbing, that's all I think, because they don't entertain at all, and get plenty to live on, no family. It's madness on her part, I think. Well, Mother, au revoir till next week. Where shall I be I wonder?

Much love to you all and kisses.

Queenie.

P.S. I never write apart to Doll because you send her my letters, of course. Love to them all. Q.

Chapter 10: To Scotland

Royal Hotel, Inverness,
18th April, 1917

Dearest Mother,

You see, it is Scotland. I went before a board on Monday. They were so kind, Miss Conyers, our Matron-in-Chief, is the whitest woman one could meet. Colonel Ryan gave me a fortnight's leave and asked me where I would go. I thought of Killarney, but he advised me not to go just now for several reasons, but I think, as he is an Irish-man, the chief reason was he thought the weather was too bad, and he said I must go and see the lakes in the summer and Miss C. advised Scotland.

Another sister is with me. She has been taken off her boat after doing ten months in the Mediterranean. No women are to stay on hospital ships on account of so many going down lately. You remember I came over on the "H.S. Salta" from Alexandria to Marseilles? Well, the ship was coming over from Havre last week, struck a loose mine and sank in three minutes. All staff, but thank God, no patients.

Well, now I must tell you from the beginning. We have a free pass right here return, so it only means our expenses and I have been saving up so am going to have a glorious time. Sister and I caught the 1.15 p.m. train at Euston on Tuesday and arrived here this morning at 5.50 a.m. came through Lancashire, saw the mills all round Rugby, Crewe, and changed at Perth. We really slept quite well. The old guard on the train looked after us like a father and we had two Cameron Highlanders (Lieutenants) with us all the way. They went on to camp at Invergarden further on. We had to have passports to pass off the station, being the Naval Base of course.

It was beautiful to see the snow on the Hielands early this morning coming through Perthshire. We had about two hours sleep, a good wash and a huge breakfast, plenty of porridge, and by 9 a.m. started out to walk to the Islands along the Caledonian Canal. It was about four miles down towards the sea and very fresh and a wee bit chilly, but when we had gone about two miles, we were warm as toast. It was the most glorious walk I've ever had. Glens so peaceful, patches of snow on the hills.

On our way, we saw the Castle and Flora McDonald's statue. The view is very good from there also, and then on our return home we went into the wonderful

Cathedral. We didn't get home till 1.30 p.m. and must have walked about eight miles. We had lunch, but did not feel equal to see Culloden Battle Field, so had a camp *(rest)*. We passed rather a quaint looking cemetery on our walk this morning, a place called "Tomnahurick", saw the stones with funny Scotch words such as "Our Wee Willie" aged eight years. Numerous McKenzies and Mc's of all descriptions.

Sister has gone to bed. We both had a hot bath and feel very tired, especially as I'm really "collar proud" after ten days in a closed room and not able to walk about. The measles seem to have been an ill wind that blew some good. I would never have had this luck as all leave is stopped. Well, we intend to leave in the 9.30 a.m. train tomorrow for Edinburgh, hoping to stay there about four or five days and then do the Trossacks and Glasgow, returning home at our leisure within the fortnight. We were so excited yesterday.

I shall write you again from Edinburgh, Mum, and if you would like to send my letters on to Coley, do. She would like to hear of my trip out of London. I feel very tired.

Much love to you all, dears, from Queenie.

The Royal Hotel, Edinburgh,
20th April, 1917.

Dearest Mother,

We arrived here yesterday at 5.30 p.m. from Inverness. Stayed about two hours in Perth, changed trains and had lunch. The Hielands were covered with snow, but the sun was out and it's beautiful weather really. We did not go anywhere but just saw the Scott's Memorial opposite the Hotel and then we met a N.Z. Officer I know, and he and another took Sister and I to "The Empire", vaudeville, etc., rather tropical, but it's all that was on. We got to bed jolly tired about 12.30 after our train journey down.

I forgot to tell you, we passed across Culloden Moor and saw the harbour or Firth from the train. Cremorty, you know where the fleet is. The walk we went the day before was down the Caledonian Canal. Scotland is so different to England somehow. Still its beauty does not make me any the less homesick for old Australia, dear to us all. Well, we bathed and breakfasted by 10 a.m. this morning and off to the castle. A guide, an old soldier, was just taking a party of Anzacs so we fell in too, and he told us great stories of Mary, Queen of Scots, and the James 1 of England. I sat in Mary's chair where James was born. The view is very beautiful from the castle. Well, we then went down to St. Giles Cathedral, which, of course, you have read about and I know all its wonders. It is just near the castle, and in the courtyard were lots of Jocks drilling doing the goose step, etc. We then did John Knox home.

By then it was nearly 1 p.m. so back we came and had lunch. This afternoon we were asked out to tea, which was very proper at a Scotch home. These people *(are)* interested in the "Colonials", you know. We had lovely scones and oatmeal cakes, so when we came back we went for a trap ride about an hour, and here I am scribbling to you. Just received a wire from Reg Sellars. It is true, poor Billie Lee is killed. Poor Uncle and Aunt. I'm so sorry for them. Very glad Reggie was with Billie, he is now on leave. I s'pose I shall try to see him.

We are going to Holyrood Palace tomorrow and either to Calendar or Glasgow in the p.m. depends on trains to suit. So must go off to sleep. Very tired and you shall hear all about the Trossacks later.

Much love and kisses to you all.

Queenie.

Dreadnought Hotel, Callender,
22nd April, 1917.

Dearest Mother,

We have seen quite a lot since I wrote you on Friday. Yesterday morning we went all through Holyrood Palace, Queen Mary's apartments, saw wonderful pictures and tapestries while the spirits of Mary, James, Lord Darnley, Charles, Bess, etc., etc., followed us from room to room. We then went up 287 steps to the top of Scotts Memorial. *(Sir Walter Scott's Memorial, erected a few years after his death 1845)* We were giddy and faint when we got down again. We then went round to see an auction sale at the Y.M.C.A. A few old Countesses and Duchesses and "Lidy's, etc., working for the Red Cross, had lunch, then left the Royal Hotel for the Station at 2.30 p.m.

Secured our tickets for a return to Crainlurich, which is at the head of Loch Katrine, but we stay here and do the Trossacks first. On our way here we saw Wallace's and Robert Bruce's Memorial, and as we had three-quarters of an hour in Stirling, we walked to the castle. What with castles and churches, we need never see any more for the rest of our lives. Still, it is all most interesting and wonderful (five hundred and six hundred years ago). All most beautiful oak (solid) inside. Well, to carry on, we arrived here at 6.30 last night, had dinner and went to bed dead tired. Oh, I must tell you we have three more sisters with us since Thursday, so we are leaving in an hour for the Trossacks, which is ten miles from Callender and our carriage and pair will be here any moment. We are taking our lunch and now I shall stop and finish this tonight so you can have my fresh impression of our drive.

10 p.m: Dead beat, but must finish our day to you. If you only saw our coachman up in a high seat and the five of us in the open laundau. J.K. Stewart's turnout not in it. Well, we drive twenty miles all along Loch Achray and through the Trossacks to the head of Loch Katrine. We should have taken the steamer then, only since the war it is not running, no coal. Well, we had lunch at the Trossacks Hotel and looked around Katrine for an hour arriving back here at 4 p.m. They tell us here it is a perfect day for the Lakes, bright sun shining and quite warm, could not have a rug across our knees, so you see we were lucky. It was very beautiful. Snow on all the hills all round and blue sky. We had a 'camp', and a bath, dressed for dinner and have not long come in from a walk thro' the glens nearby. It is a pretty place. We are off in the morning for Crainburich.

Love Queenie.

P.S. Saw the Battle of Bannockburn the other side of Stirling.

Caledonian Railway Company,
Central Station Hotel,
Glasgow, Tuesday night.

Well Mum, I'm dead tired, but as these last two days have been the best, I must tell you about it. We left Callender on Monday morning, and had a very pretty train journey to "Crainburich" where we passed Loch Earn and the end of Loch Tay and some very pretty glens. We could not get a train to Tarbet till 7.30 p.m. so we asked the station master to let us go down on a goods train, and he did. Well, the forty minutes in the van was perfect, we were alongside Loch Lomond and all the way, and arrived at Tarbet at 4 p.m. Weather bright and sunny, best I've seen since in England. The reflections on the Loch, waves without wind, fish without fins and a floating island are all to be seen. I don't think!

However, we had tea, of course, we had lunch at Crainburich, I forgot to tell you we eat sometimes and not much either, they are cutting the food down very much. We walked along the "bonnie banks" last evening and played Bridge with a Scotch soldier in the lounge at night. Started at 10 p.m. Lights go out at 10.30, so we didn't play for long and we were tired too. The sun and fresh air make me very drowsy. Well, this morning we got up at 8.30 a.m. bathed, which we pay one shilling for. Had breakfast, also must tell you it has been the same ever since I left Southall. Porridge, bacon and eggs and oatmeal biscuits. Sick of the look of it all too. Well, we hired a motor, the first run since we started really, and we motored up to the top of the hills called 'The Rest and be Thankful', 1814, where the Gordon Highlanders rested after some battle. It was bonnie sailing through the sharp air with the sun shining. We took off our hats. We only went twenty miles, ten there and ten back, as it is one shilling a mile and four shillings each was quite enough, but it was worth it. We went all along Loch Long and saw a torpedo station there and we were an awful way up in the Hielands.

We got back in time to square up our bill and pack up our small suit cases which we carry ourselves to save tips, and then join the steamer at 12 p. m. for Inversnaid up the Loch again. Stayed two hours, had lunch and saw some falls. We then left for Ballock, passing Tarbet again and arriving at Ballock 4.30 p.m. all that time on Loch Lomond. All sunburnt and dead beat. We have had dinner and train ride and now feel like the 'rest and be thankful'. I am going to keep an account of every penny and tell you how much it has cost me. So far I have spent six pounds, eight shillings – you see, we have been careful. This is a huge shipping centre and not very interesting, so am leaving for London in the morning.

To bed and now to sleep. Much love and kisses. Queenie.

P.S. Do send my trip to Coley.

Chapter 11: Southall

Southall
8th May, 1917

Dearest Mother, and all at home,

Your letters are coming very regularly lately, and I send them all on to Andy. I have not heard from him lately so do not know if he has gone to France, but expect news from him any day. I am quite settled down now after my trip and on duty in another ward. We are not at all busy, plenty of Sisters waiting to go to France. Miss Conyers, our Matron-in-Chief was very nice to me when I reported at headquarters after my leave, and said I was to come back here again. So perhaps I won't go to France for yet awhile.

It's such glorious weather, the boys are calling me to come out and get snapped with them, eight boys without legs at all, and they have a wheel chair and go all over the place. I'm so glad Jim has enlisted, Mother, before you got my letter telling him to do so and asking you if you could manage to live. He will be glad afterwards and when he gets over here, Mum I will look after him. Andy is different and can take care of himself, but Jim and I will have more love for each other and I can arrange for him to come here on leave and go down and see him at Salisbury. So you need not worry about us and when we come home what a great time we will have even if we have to eat worms.

(Page missing)

And haven't a sou. I hope you will get my letters from Scotland and I sent Len a guide of Edinborough Castle. I'm awfully glad he is trying for the Jervis Bay *(Royal Australian Naval College).* It is the highest thing a man can do in life, the Navy is great and no one would be prouder than I, if he gets through. When he goes to Brisbane, Mum, get someone influential, say McLennon M.P., to meet and take him to the Medical Officer; it is only influence everywhere.

I went to a very swagger dinner party the other day at the Langham Hotel and on our way we saw Queen Alexandra step into her carriage from the Queen's Hall. She was present at some charity concert. We thought it was a wedding at first with the crowds, but a yell of "The Queen, The Queen" and of course we felt then we were in the presence of Royalty. A Mrs Alexander gave this dinner party and afterwards we went to see "The Old Lady Shows Her Medals" at the New Theatre. Three different comedies by "Barrie". Irene Vanburgh is very good. This Mrs Alexander was a charming old lady like Queen Victoria in figure, dressed in black velvet and gorgeous diamonds. She has four Australian officers always at her home in Surrey, legless men. Well, we know two of them so, she asked us to dinner with them. Wasn't it nice of her, and they are her guests at The Langham while they are getting their limbs fitted at Roehampton.

Now they have gone back to Capsley and she has written and asked us down. We might go if the cash can stand it. I'm not very keen on these big country homes. They *(the officers)* get bored to tears with themselves, only the boys are awfully nice. One is a Mr. Falconer of Toowoomba and knows Len Lee, very young and his leg off at the hip. I send Andy your letters at once and when he gets his commission in France, will send him several things. He says he has met some nice English friends, but I am telling him to be careful, one can't trust mere acquaintances in the army and the English girls are only out to catch our men. I have some socks now for him when I get his new address.

Poor old Doll and her babies. I don't think I shall ever get married. I'd love to have children but what's the good if you live in a deadly hole and no fun? After the war we will have no choice if we haven't caught a husband now, will we? Never mind, I'm strong and refuse to be an old maid, nobody wants them.

Poor Billie Lee had his arm blown off and bled to death in a few minutes. Reggie Sellars wrote and told me. Auntie Susie will be very upset. Tell Jim if it is not too late, to try and get into the heavy artillery. The casualties are not so big and are some distance back from the front trenches, of course when they get hit, it's a good one, but I know lots of boys, Bill Cowton one of them, they are still going hard in France and not wounded. He ought to be coming over on leave again soon.

Bert Norris wrote and said he would be over next week. I must be a queer sort of girl, I think. He is very keen, but I can't care enough for him. However, some day things might change. You know, Mother, when he was in England six months ago, I was on my way in a taxi to Horseferry Road, to make arrangements to be married and changed my mind before we got there. Poor Bert!. But don't say a word of this to anyone will you?

I had better stop this epistle, I don't often tell you my love affairs, they are too numerous and humorous. You would get mixed up in them, and before I get too sentimental, will say au revoir and much love to you all dears,

Queenie.

P.S. Tell Len to study hard for the Naval Exam. I would love him to go there. Q.

Southall, 15th May, 1917.

Dearest Mum and all at home,

The mail closes tonight although I never really worry, but write every week. Do you notice the dates? I think we miss occasional letters from you, but still I always seem to get more home letters than most of the sisters.

I must tell you I had my day off last week on Saturday and spent it with Colin Cameron, Bert Norris and Simon Porter from Eaton. Colin and Simon have fleshy wounds and are now convalescent, while Bert is on leave for ten days. He is in the 9th Battalion and they were in the firing lines till hardly any left and then brought out and those that were not wounded, given ten days leave. Doesn't it seem awful, eight officers killed in a small attack? And poor old Colin had just received a cable from Jessie to say his father had passed away, so we kept him with us all day, had lunch at The Trocadero and made him come to the Colliseum in the afternoon.

Mary Anderson acts in Pygmalion and Galatea with Lady Tree. It was a very good show really; we then had tea at the Piccadilly restaurant, walked through Hyde Park, then had dinner and they brought us home. I had a Sister Stevenson with me. We call her 'Steve'. Well, then I worked all day Sunday till 8 p.m. from 6 a.m. and then yesterday Steve and I had a glorious day in Surrey.

I must tell you all about it. Steve has a friend there who takes Australian officers with legs off during their convalescence and waiting for artificial limbs. Well, we thought our Sgt. Wilson, would love a week or so there too, so Mrs. Alexander said she would have him and arranged for us to take him down. We taxied at her expense to Hampton Court, nine miles from here and they met us with their car. We started at 9.30 a.m. and got to Hampton Court at 10 a.m., went through the Palace, Maze and Gardens which are beautiful just now and off we started at 11 a.m. for Capsley, twenty-seven miles away through most beautiful country. I daresay you know it well.

We stopped on the Common where Lloyd George plays golf and lives just near and we had lemonade and biscuits. We arrived at Capsley at 12 p. m. It was a "tres bon" run alright and Lieutenant Falconer, who drove, has just had his wooden leg a fortnight and comes from Toowoomba and knows Len Lee well. Isn't it funny meeting people like that? The old lady was very charming. We had dinner with her at The Langham, I think I told you before. She fussed over the Sergeant and took him quite out of our care at once. He is such a dear boy, Mum, and never murmurs and wears his two legs all day, walks very well.

We took several snaps on the terrace and lawn, so will send some to you. We will miss him very much as he was three months in my ward. They had two lovely big Collie dogs, I raced around the lawn with them.

Well, we left Capsley at 6 p.m. and arrived Victoria 7 p.m., met Bert and Colin again and had dinner at a French café in Soho. You will think we are very gay and not doing our bit, but I don't tell you much of the war or wards. I have to work all day this week now, but we are not at all busy. Bert leaves for Scotland today and Colin goes to Digswell House Convalescent Hospital for Australian Officers, so our little flutter is over.

Bert says it's only a matter of time and they will all be killed, but it's awful to hear them say these things and we know it's only too true. I have not heard from Andy for three weeks. He must be in France and I do wish he would write and let me know where he is. I am writing to Headquarters about him.

Had a letter from George Cole, he is very well and sent me his Mum's letter. I shall write to Doll this week. Much love to you all and kisses...I wonder is Jim in camp yet?

xxxx Queen.

Sgt Ivor Wilson, a double amputee visiting Mrs Alexander's, Capsley UK, May 1917.

Southall,
10th June, 1917.

Dearest Mum and all at home,

Another week gone by and still no news of Andy, all I hope is you are getting letters from him. I am not worrying because they say at Headquarters he's alright. Well, it's quite three weeks since the Australian mail came in. I expect to get three or four letters from you. The weather is very hot and muggy and I can guess what it is like in London. I feel it a lot more than Queensland heat. I am not going into London for some time, am too fagged and tired out. We have all been inocculated and it has played up horribly, we are not the fresh creatures of two years ago. I am having another injection tomorrow night. Its horrid stuff, makes us squarmish, similar to seasick.

I took two of my stumpy boys to London yesterday afternoon and I feel quite knocked out. They wanted to come shopping with me and I had to get Jack Earwaker some things so they came too. We shopped at Selfridges, a huge American shop, and it is beautiful inside, then we had tea with a good string band and I took them round and through Hyde Park for a half hour in a taxi. It is really on the way to Paddington. I can't do much, never have the cash, but they enjoyed themselves. One was an Innisfail boy, Geof Greer, and he is going back on the next boat.

Last Saturday afternoon another sister and myself took the real stumpy's (boys without legs at all), to the cricket match at Uxbridge, our orderlies against the Canadians. The colonel gave us a car *(charabanc, a large bus for sightseeing, usually open topped)*, and quite twenty came and we sat on the lawn and cheered and backed our boys. They loved it. Plenty of "Say no" from the Canadians, of course. We are going to the woods for a picnic one day if the C.O. will give us the car.

I really can't believe the news this week. Matron says all the sisters are to go on leave for this year, and I said, "Oh, I've had mine", and she said that was only sick leave after measles, so what do you think of me off for another fortnight? I am going with Sister Myrtle Cooper to Killarney and Llandudno, if funds will allow.

We get a concession on railway and could stay four days in Killarney and ten in Wales, but until there, don't you believe it, because it seems too good. I shall write to you every day if I do go. It will be more beautiful than Scotland, don't you think? I loved Loch Lomond and Tarbet and also Inverness. Still, I might not be able to go to Killarney yet. We can bathe at Llanludno and the band plays on the pier every evening.

I have a sweet dinner frock, Georgette and glace black, very smart, but you must think me very selfish, always writing of my doings, although I know you like hearing all my travels. I might as well see all I can now. We haven't much money, but we do see "Life". I have learnt to foxtrot: one step and hesitate, so I expect to have a gay holiday. I went on the Thames at Richmond one afternoon last week. It's not far from here, catch a bus from Ealing Broadway. I sat back while a very nice Major punted up stream. Had dinner at a hotel on the river and a cig after on the lawn, then glided down. It was so cool and so gay, as you know, all kinds of boats and people and frocks and parasols out. It really is very good weather, I should think for England, quite a drought, but very muggy.

(Rest of letter missing)

Chapter 12: Return to Brisbane

Queenie's letters from June 1917 to 2nd October, 1917 are missing, so we will never know how the holiday to Wales and Ireland went, but it is certain Queenie and her travelling companion, Sister Myrtle Cooper, will have seen the sights, spent as little money as possible and enjoyed themselves immensely.

Queenie embarked on the hospital transport Euripides on 21st July, 1917, bound for home, nursing wounded soldiers. She was meant to return to England with outbound troops, but her orders were delayed several times. In the interim, she nursed at No. 6 Australian General Hospital at Kangaroo Point, in a building later to house the migrant hostel.

Brisbane, Queensland, Australia,
2nd October, 1917.

Dearest Mother and family,

I am still here and likely to be for a while. We were all ready to go to Sydney, but postponed at the last minute, so I am not going to think of going. Matron thinks it will be next week. I have a day off-duty tomorrow and going out to Coley's tonight to sleep, but coming back at midday tomorrow as I promised to go with the troops to Oxley on a motor trip. I took a number of returned soldiers down to Mrs Bond's Sen. for an afternoon party last Wednesday. Coley, Mrs Earwaker, Mrs Markwell and Mrs Ivor Bond were there to entertain them. They loved them all and the boys had a good time.

Have no official news of my second star so far, but I think it's pretty sure. Matron wouldn't tell me if not. I have a ward of five boys now. It is mauve and pale pink and looks so nice. I wish you could come and see it. Coley came over yesterday afternoon and talked to my soldiers and Mrs Earwaker has adopted one for the time being, comes every other day to see him, brought him a beautiful big bunch of poppies today.

Grandad came over this morning to see me and had a yarn to 'the boys' while I was with the Captain. He is alright. I told him you said you would come south as soon as you could get away and he only wishes you would. Am glad to hear your friends have cheered you up. I would rather you came down to Sydney than Brisbane. It's deadly slow here, not a show worth going to. Still, there is Len's education. I don't think he can transfer to Sydney. I like Brisbane, of course. I've heard from the "Quartette" often, they are waiting for me to come down. I will wire you when I do leave here, Mum. It's horrid waiting and trying to keep the laundry clean.

Heaps of love to you all and kisses to Doll and the babies.

Queenie.

P.S. I was going to ask Mr Ferricks to try and get my second pip, but blow them. I'd better not have anything to do with them at all, in fact, I haven't seen them since I returned. Q.

Editor's note: Mr. Miles Aloysius Ferricks was Dolly's brother-in-law, (married to Ken Waugh's sister), and at that time was an ALP Senator in the Australian Federal Parliament. Thank you to Dolly's grandson, Les Whelan, Camp Hill, Brisbane, for this item of information.

Pat Richardson

No. 6 Australian General Hospital, Brisbane,
9th October, 1917.

Dearest Mother and all at home,

This is my third day on duty and I feel so tired, the hours seem longer than abroad, but I s'pose I am a bit collar-proud. Well, we were all very disappointed with the "Tango Maru" and all the travellers said the inter-state boats were much nicer. The waiting was rotten and the lavatories and bathrooms dirty. The food was very off, so don't come on one of them when you think of leaving Townsville. "Canberra" and "Wyandra" are the best. All our luggage was put on the wharf and searched on account of the east trading.

I have not been out yet. Had a morning in town, met Coley and went out to Elsvick for dinner. We lunched at Rowes and met lots of people I knew. Gerty Kelling looking much older and her little girl Mary. She is in a good position in Brisbane. She was so glad to see me and said Douglas was over at the Front and she would like her mother to meet me etc., etc., and Mrs Stryinger, now Mrs Ward, looking twenty years younger, lunching at Rowes with her new husband. Coley said she could not get a moment with me.

I have not been out since, but have had several visitors over to see me. Leslie Byers came last night. He is discharged and is now a Crown's Land Manager at Roma. Only a young man of twenty-five, so he's doing well. We were in Egypt together. I'm going out to have tea at the Cooee tomorrow with him. Lieutenant Phillips is coming over tonight. We met in England, he is also discharged and an accountant in the Queensland Bank.

I do not know how long I will be here, but I wish you were near. A nice house next door to ours, (we are billeted in houses), is only one pound per week rent, gas and verandah all round. Beautiful garden and very pretty view of the river. Of course, people are in it, but I was thinking of you up there in the back of beyond. I do wish you would come down here, Mother. I am in charge of a very nice ward, mostly recruits being fixed up with ops for hernias.

I hope poor old Doll and the Babies are alright. Gladys Waugh rang me today, wants to come over and very anxious to see me.

(Page missing.)

No 6. Australian General Hospital,
Kangaroo Point, Brisbane,
25th October, 1917.

Dearest Mother and boys and Doll,

My departure is put off for twelve days, it is rather a good thing, as I had applied for my promotion and it would hardly have time to get through. And also the Matron-in-Chief of all sisters in the A.I.F. is up here on an official visit and Matron of this hospital told me this morning it is almost certain that I sail with my two stars up. She must have put in a good word for me, I'm sure.

Old Mrs Bond had arranged a farewell party yesterday for me. I was taking six soldiers down, all the family were coming to help entertain them, but in the morning a cable came through to say Captain Sid Bond had been killed, so it is postponed. They are all very sad, of course. Mrs Earwaker has bought me a new cabin trunk. Mine was beyond a fresh journey. She gave me two guineas and I said I would buy a box with it, but she rang up later to say Mr E. would get me a trunk at Perry's, so we got it yesterday afternoon, a beauty, stronger than my last one, must have cost a fiver.

I am taking parcels back for Jack, Tom and George, also Lottie Bond's husband, who is wounded. Poor old Bert Norris is severely wounded. I hope he is doing well and has not lost any limbs. We had a very nice Lucinda trip last Saturday, no one took any notice of the Premier and his wife, but it was quite nice, the band played. I sent you Andy's letter, not much news, but it's good to hear from him.

I am going in charge of our transport and the boat is still at the Bulimba Wharf, but we embark in Sydney. It is very hot today, dusty and muggy. I pass Coley's house going down to the ferry, it is just opposite gas? and only nineteen shillings and sixpence week rent. People are in it, of course, but is so near Queen Street and yet on the river. I like Kangaroo Point myself, also Ascot along the river.

I wish you were down near me all these weeks, but I know it is not to be. The "Koopa" trots up and down the river, it is quite busy. The "Demosthenes", "Euripides", and "Nestor', (Hospital Ships), are all in at the Bulimba wharf. I often see Mrs Short and Norma in the street. They spoke to me once, bit I didn't encourage them, so we just smile at each other. Met Mrs Hawthorne in my ward doing Red Cross work. I went out to Coley's, she is a dear soul and I hope I see Tom and George.

The casualty list is big this time. Quite a number of returned boys arrive tomorrow afternoon. I guess I shall know quite a number. I packed all ready to leave today. Thanks so much for darning my woollies. They will be used on arrival in London, eh! what! And my kimono is just nice for the boat and special occasions after. I bought two pairs of boots, corsets, and singlets for my new journey. Hope we won't be submarined and lose all my outfits, especially my new box. Well, Mum, I shall write again from Sydney.

Take care of your dear selves. I'm always thinking of you all and only wished you were down here, but just write to us every week.

Much love and kisses, send this on to Doll. I hope she is alright.

Queenie.

This is the last letter found.

Despite expecting to return to England, Queenie's orders are changed and she is allocated to the AANS's home service with No. 6 Australian General Hospital at Kangaroo Point, Brisbane. The following year, on 24th September 1918, she contracted ptomaine poisoning – a not uncommon cause of death in the days before regulated food preservation – and spent more than three months in hospital. The doctor's signature on one of her medical reports is that of Harvey Walsh, a handsome, dark haired man who had served on transports during the war. He saved her life, they fell in love at her bedside and they married when she regained her health.

Harvey Sylvester Walsh had enlisted at the age of twenty-seven on 22nd November, 1916. Appointed medical officer with the rank of Captain in the AIF Transport Service, he embarked from Sydney aboard HMAT *Demosthenes* exactly a month later, on 22nd December. Arriving at Plymouth on 3rd March, 1917, he returned to Australia aboard hospital transport vessel *Barambah* on 8th April and reported for duty at No. 6 Australian General Hospital at Kangaroo Point. The building was later to serve as a migrant centre.

Almost two years later, on 14th January, 1919, as the doctor in charge of Queenie's case, he was to write in a report on the patient with whom he may already have been in love: "Contracted acute ptomaine poisoning whilst on nursing duties at 6 A.G.H. ... three abdominal incisions were made on two separate occasions in endeavours to locate abscess but without success. Abscess later ruptured into bowel and discharged. Patient was in bed for three and a half months." The report notes: "Patient is now convalescent and sitting up – is very thin and weak and at present quite unable to walk".

It was not perhaps the most romantic setting for a courtship, but it worked for Queenie and Harvey. Discharged from hospital and the Australian Army Nursing Service on 17th January, 1919, just three days after Harvey Walsh's medical report, Queenie was still very weak and took several more months to fully regain her health. Her mother, Matilda, "Tilly", meanwhile, had moved from Townsville to Sydney with Queenie's younger brothers, Jim, Bob and Len. Queenie likely lived with them until her marriage to Harvey, as the marriage certificate gives Darlinghurst as her home.

Dr Harvey Walsh is said by his daughter, Rosslyn Héro, to have saved her mother's life when she contracted ptomaine poisoning in Brisbane while serving at No. 6 Australian General Hospital.

Queenie and Harvey were married in October 1919 at St. Stephen's Cathedral in Brisbane. She was then twenty-nine and he was thirty. They may have met before the war in Bowen in North Queensland, where her father had been the local head master and where he was born. After their marriage, the couple lived in Enoggera Terrace, Red Hill, Brisbane, where Dr Walsh went into private practice and Queenie, after years of active service healing horrific wounds and helping to rehabilitate soldiers who had suffered amputations, became a doctor's surgery nurse in suburban Brisbane and raised their two children, Rosslyn and Richard. It would have been a busy, contented time: Queenie lived a very active social life, playing bridge and golf, and the Walshes were often mentioned in the social pages as being seen at the theatre, or holidaying at Southport.

On 23rd October, 1936, Queenie died suddenly from a cerebral haemorrhage and heart failure after a game of golf at the Brisbane Golf Club. She was just forty-six years old. A grief-stricken Harvey Walsh suffered a nervous breakdown and their two children were sent more or less permanently to boarding school. The family home was sold and, as a result, very little of Queenie's wartime memorabilia survived except some of her letters and her precious photograph album. It was an abrupt and tragic end to the life of a woman who had been a hardworking country hospital matron, a dedicated wartime nurse and a loving wife and mother.

Right: A short article about Queenie's death on 23rd October, 1936, was published in the Courier Mail, Brisbane.

Left: Queenie always wore the latest fashions of the day

Sudden Death of Mrs. Harvey Walsh

Many friends, particularly in golfing circles, will grieve to hear of the death of Mrs. Harvey S Walsh, which occurred at her home, Enoggera Terrace, Red Hill, late last night. The late Mrs. Walsh, who was a keen golfer, and who had been an associate of the Brisbane Golf Club for the past 10 years, played at Yeerongpilly yesterday afternoon, and returned home apparently in the best of health. Later in the evening however, she suffered a seizure, from which she never rallied.

LATE MRS. HARVEY WALSH.

A daughter of the late Mr. R. G. Avenell and of Mrs. Avenell, Brisbane, Mrs. Walsh was born in Gympie and was trained as a nurse in the Mackay Hospital. For four years, during the Great War, she saw service both in France and Egypt. On her return to Queensland she married in 1919 Dr. Harvey S. Walsh, by whom she is survived. She also leaves two children, Roslyn, aged 13, who is a pupil at Stuartholme Convent, and Dick, a son of 11.

The funeral, which will be private, will leave the Rosalie Roman Catholic Church this afternoon for the Toowong Cemetery.

Appendix 1: Notes on Chapter 1

Notes on the nurses and soldiers mentioned in Chapter 1:

Queenie remained in touch throughout the war with **Sister Echlin**, whom she mentions in her first letter home in May 1915. Gladys Ivy "Daisy" Echlin enlisted in November 1914 and was in the first group of Army nurses to embark for Egypt on the Kyarra, which sailed from Australia on 21st November, 1914. Queenie and Daisy met often in Cairo and they later spent time together in London. Twenty-seven years old on her enlistment, Daisy Echlin was born in Bulimba, Queensland and trained at the Brisbane General Hospital; her father had served in the Boer War and her parents lived in Gatton.

According to her service record, she also had nursed in Mackay and she and Queenie may have known each other there before the war. Daisy Echlin served in Egypt, England and France, returning to Australia with wounded soldiers in January 1916. In July, 1917 she was awarded the Royal Red Cross, 2nd Class. Her friendship with Queenie may have endured after the war as both lived in Brisbane and attended the same events on occasion; they both attended a reunion of returned nurses at Rowes, Brisbane on 25th November, 1932. Daisy Echlin died in Brisbane on 2nd September, 1971, aged eighty-four.

ECHLIN, Gladys Ivy (Daisy) ARRC. Returned Sister World War 1.

On September 2nd. Elder Daughter of the late Capt. and Mrs R. B. Echlin and dearest Sister of Warren (England) and Nancy Feid. Privately cremated September 3rd.

Sister Echlin's death notice and photo.

Frederick Anthony James Waldon Taylor, a Brisbane wool valuer, enlisted on the 18th of September, 1914 and served in Gallipoli, Egypt and the Middle East with the 5th Light Horse Regiment. The former Brisbane Grammar School cadet rose to the rank of Lieutenant, was mentioned in despatches and, in October 1917, seconded as ADC to General Sir Edmund Allenby who led the Palestine campaign. He was awarded the Order of the Nile, Fourth Class, by the Sultan of Egypt. Waldon Taylor survived the war and returned to Australia, living to the age of eighty-six.

Frederick Eckersley Boddington was not so lucky. Enlisting at Helena Vale, in Western Australia on August 17, 1914, the Maryborough-born architect and civil engineer served with the 11th Battalion at Gallipoli, later transferring to the 46th Battalion. He was killed in action on 11th April, 1917, on the first day of the battalion's attack on the Hindenburg Line in the Battle of Bullecourt.

Trooper Edward Homer Williams was a twenty-nine-year-old grazier from the Mackay region when he was assigned to the 5th Light Horse Regiment on 23rd October, 1914. He was one of twenty-three men killed amid heavy machine gun fire during the regiment's first major operation, an attack on the Turkish-held Balkan Gun Pits on 28th June, 1915 in an action meant to prevent the Turks diverting forces to meet an attack at Cape Helles. Edward Williams was buried in Wright's Gully Cemetery, but his remains were later re-interred at Shell Green Cemetery.

Rockhampton-born grazier **Frederick Young Fox** enlisted on 4th September, 1914 aged just twenty. He saw service with the 9th Battalion at Gallipoli and later served in France with the 49th Battalion where he was promoted to the rank of Captain in 1917 and again wounded in action. He returned to Australia in October 1918 after four years of war.

Alexander Campbell Cunningham was a Lance Corporal with the Ceylon Planters Rifle Corps at the outbreak of war, later transferring to the British Army's Royal Munster Fusiliers, "The Incomparables", as a 2nd Lieutenant. He landed with his regiment at Suvla Bay in August 1915 and was part of an attack on Scimitar Hill on the 21st, during which the Turks set fire to the scrub between the two forces. It was high summer and the prickly holly scrub was dry as tinder. Many of the wounded were unable to escape the raging blaze and Lieutenant Cunningham was one of many officers killed that day.

Queensland nursing Sister **Ellen Chidgey** was thirty-three years old when she enlisted in the Australian Army Nursing Service on 31st July, 1915. She served in Egypt and England but was forced to resign on her marriage on 9th December, 1916 – army rules were that a nurse was no longer retained once she married, although rare exceptions were permitted.

Mary Jane Derrer's Military Medal for courage under fire was still ahead of her when she and Queenie met up on the dusty streets of Cairo in 1915. Two years later, on 22nd July, 1917, Sister Derrer was one of four nurses at No. 2 Casualty Clearing Station at Trois Arbres in France when it came under a German bombing attack. Despite pleas from their patients to save themselves, the four nurses carried the wounded men from the collapsed tents and tried to shelter them from harm by covering their heads with metal basins and placing tables over their beds. Sister Derrer, Dorothy Cawood, Clare Deacon and Alice Ross King were the first four Australian nurses to receive the Military Medal "for bravery in the field"; in all, eight Australian nurses received the award during the war.

Ross Burrell was a twenty-four-year-old accountant from Townsville who was assigned to the 2nd Light Horse Regiment Field Hospital when he enlisted on 26th October, 1914. He was wounded at Gallipoli and later served with the 5th Australian Field Ambulance in France, where he was promoted to Sergeant. He was discharged in May 1918 after a gunshot wound to his face.

John George (Jack) Earwaker was just eighteen when he enlisted on 29th June, 1915. He served at Gallipoli with 9th Battalion and, despite his youth, rose through the ranks and was appointed Lieutenant on 1st December, 1917. Just over nine months later, he was awarded the Military Cross for "his cool judgement and utter disregard for his personal safety" during an advance at Villeret , in France, on 18th September, 1918.

When Queenie met up with him again in London in 1916, Lieutenant **Herbert Lionel Norris** of the Queensland 9th Battalion was a little under a year away from earning the Military Cross for his bravery on 29th September, 1917, at in Glencourse Wood near Hooge in Belgium. The citation in the London Gazette reads in part: "This officer's splendid courage and determination in advancing after being severely wounded set a fine example to his men. The gallant conduct and initiative shown by him during the advance proved him to be a leader of sterling qualities." The wound was so severe it disabled his left arm and Lieutenant Norris left England to return home on 1st February, 1918.

Appendix 2: Major Harry William Lee

The Lee men, Maryborough, Queensland. Colonel H.W. Lee. Headmaster, Maryborough, South-East Queensland. He also commanded the Wide Bay Militia and on April 25, 1915, commanded the 9th Battalion at the landing at Gallipoli. Captain H.W. Lee, (Billie or Willie). He was killed in action in France on 20th March, 1917. Billie's younger brother Clive Lee is in cadet's uniform. Sergeant Major Harry Lee, seated, served in the Crimea and retired to Australia. Photo taken about 1912.

Courtesy of Dick Monks, Naremburn, Sydney.

"Tell them I died gamely," were the young officer's last words as his blood ebbed into the French soil. Major Harry William "Billie" Lee was just twenty-five years old when he was commanding the 25th Battalion near Vaulx-Vraucourt on 20th March, 1917. He was siting machine gun positions under enemy artillery fire when a shell tore into his body. His comrades rushed him to the Battalion Aid Post but nothing could be done to save him. Billie Lee died of a massive loss of blood half an hour later.

Born on 14th May, 1892, the articled law clerk and former Maryborough State School student was just twenty-two years old when he enlisted in the Australian Imperial Force as a Captain. Assigned to the 9th Battalion under the command of his father, Colonel Harry William Lee (snr), Captain Lee was designated the battalion's transport officer and embarked for Egypt aboard the troop ship Omrah, leaving Brisbane on 24th September, 1914.

As transport officer, Captain Lee had the task of disembarking the battalion's horses, transporting them by train to Cairo and then onto Mena Camp, near the Pyramids, then acclimatising them to the region and getting them used to the fodder. After a bout of jaundice in October, 1915, he was transferred from Alexandria to Cairo, then early the following year he joined 49th Battalion. Promoted to Major, he was later to serve in 4th Pioneer Battalion before being selected for the officers' school at Aldershot, England, where he distinguished himself as a star student. Wrote his commanding officer described him as "...an officer of great determination, cheerful in disposition, quick at learning (and a) good imagination. He is fit to command a battalion in France."

On 25th January, 1917, Major Billie Lee was attached to 25th Battalion and sent to the Somme. The battalion was raised at Enoggera, Queensland, in March 1915 as part of the 7th Brigade. After fighting at Gallipoli, the 25th was the first battalion to land in France, disembarking at Marseilles on 19th March, 1916. Now part of the 2nd Division, the battalion suffered heavy casualties in the Battle of Pozieres.

When Major Lee became the battalion second in command, under Lieutenant Colonel Edward Creer Norrie, the 25th was at Mericourt, near Albert, in the Somme valley. The following month they were near Bullecourt and on 20th March came the orders to move up to Vaulx-Vraucourt as support to the advance on Noreuil. Major Lee is recorded in the battalion's diary as being killed on that day. According to a statement in his file, he "... received several nasty shell wounds about the body and died within half an hour". He is buried in Aichet Le Grand Communal Cemetery Extension, near Bapaume.

The 25th Battalion later fought near Flers in the Somme Valley, at Bullecourt, then, in September 1917, played a major role in the Battle of Menin Road and Broodseinde Ridge in Belgium. In 1918 the 25th combated the German Spring offensive before participating in battles at Morlancourt, Hamel, Amiens and in the

Somme Valley. In its final attack on 3rd October, the battalion broke the German defences at Beaurevoir and was disbanded nine days later when the guns finally fell silent, on 11th November, 1918.

Below are two letters written to Billie Lee's grief-stricken parents, Lieutenant Colonel Harry Lee and his wife, Susan:

France, 3rd April, 1917.

My Dear Colonel,

It is with a very sad heart that I sit down to write you these few lines on behalf of myself, Officers, N.C.Os and men of the 25th Battalion. The loss of your son, our second in Command, was one which has touched us all most deeply – everyone had the highest respect for him both as a soldier and a man – personally, I was delighted to be associated with such a keen soldier and fine man.

The Major died a soldier's death – he was in command of the Battalion at the time and at the time of receiving his wound was out siting machine gun positions near Vaulx-Vraucourt. The poor chap died at the Battalion Aid Post, but before dying, his last words were, "Tell them I died gamely". He was buried in the church yard of Vraucourt and our boys saw to it that the grave was attended to.

Will you please accept our most sincere sympathy in your sad loss and convey same to Mrs. Lee and family.

Yours most sincerely,

Edward Creer Norrie Lt. Col.

On behalf of the Officers, N.C.Os and men of the Battalion.

4. Anzac Section 3rd Echelon G.H.Q.

British Expeditionary Force,

2nd May, 1917.

Dear Colonel Lee,

It was with the deepest regret that I learned yesterday of the death of your son "Billy" (as he would always insist on being called).

He was one of the best and wherever he went I am sure that all who came in contact with him are of this opinion. Never can I forget all his goodness toward me.

Nothing was ever a trouble to him even if the same was a loss to himself, and the many friends that he made amongst the Sporting Fraternity in Egypt will be deeply grieved to hear of his death.

May I offer you my deepest sympathy in your great loss and express the hope that you may derive some consolation from the fact he died doing his best in a cause we all believe to be just.

Believe me to be,

Sincerely yours,

Arthur Langford.

W.A.Langford. Sgt. No. 11, (late 3rd Infantry Brigade Headquarters A.I.F.)

Appendix 3: Uncle Andy and the Avenell family

Born in Gympie, Queensland, Queenie's older brother, Andrew Richard Avenell enlisted in the Australian Imperial Force at Newcastle on 10th June, 1916. He was allotted Army number 28944 and the rank of Gunner and embarked at Sydney for England with the 3rd Reinforcements, Medium Trench Mortar Battery, aboard HMAT 'Borda' on 17th October 1916.

Disembarking at Plymouth on 9th January, 1917, Gunner Avenell was taken on strength of the 9th Training Battalion on 6th February, 1917. He was transferred to the 3rd Heavy Trench Mortar Battery on 2nd April and left for France on 16th July 1917, where he was assigned to the base depot at Touelles. Later that year, on 3rd October, he was transferred to the 5th Trench Mortar Brigade.

Andy Avenell survived the war without injury, enduring only a short period of illness before returning to England after the Armistice, where he joined Administrative Headquarters, London, on 20th December, 1918. He was later transferred to Number 2 Group on 11th June, 1919 and embarked for Australia aboard HT 'Frankfurt' on 1st July, 1919. He disembarked at Melbourne on 20th August, 1919 and was discharged at Sydney on 5th October, 1919.

Medals issued: British War Medal and the Victory Medal.

He also enlisted at the beginning of the Second World War, serving in Sydney in the Army Pay Corps at HQ Eastern Command from March 1940 to finally as Staff Sergeant. He was discharged on 1st September, 1944.

Uncle Andy was the "Black Sheep" of the family! He was my favourite uncle, of course – the rest were very respectable and hard working bank clerks and school teachers, but Uncle Andy pencilled for the bookies at the race course on Saturday afternoons. He earned as much in one afternoon as a working man would earn working for a whole week in an ordinary job. He was very quick with figures and had beautiful handwriting.

His service during the Second World War did not preclude his pencilling on Saturday afternoons at the Sydney racetracks. At one stage the army was going to promote him, but then found he might not have Saturday afternoons off, so he gave that idea away.

Uncle Andy returned from his service in the First World War and announced that 'only fools and horses worked! He always dressed beautifully in a suit and was very well spoken. He was actually supporting his second wife Betty, plus her father, plus Betty's teenage niece and often her sister and her three children, and an absolute menagerie of animals during the Second World War at a rented semi in Maroubra. For the life of me I can't remember where we all fitted – I stayed with them when my mother was very ill and every night we played rummy and poker around a big dining room table, as well as Lotto (Bingo).

Unfortunately, the photo of Queenie and Andy, which she mentions she is getting taken while they were in London, does not survive, and I have no family photos of him when he was a young man. He had 'shot-through' very early from the family and doesn't appear in the photograph at Dolly's wedding in Bowen in 1912. He was always well over fifty in any photos I have of him. He had the Avenell nose – rather large and red, however, he was a teetotaller and his looks belied his abstemious habits. He always was very grand of manner and had 'no time for the workers'!

He adored me too, so it was a mutual admiration society!

Pat Richardson

Queenie's mother, Matilda Jane Avenell née Lee and Andy Avenell, 1920s, Sydney.

Queenie's mother, Matilda Jane Lee, was born Buttevant, Cork, Ireland in a British Army Base, 29th June, 1862. Married in St. Pauls, Southwark, London on 6th August, 1882 and died in Sydney, aged seventy-eight, on 12th January, 1941.

Queenie's father, Richard Goodall Avenell, was born Farnham, Surrey, England on 10th December 1860 and died Bowen, North Queensland, Australia, on 7th May, 1914 (drowned in the Bowen Baths.) They had migrated to Australia as school teachers to the Colony of Queensland in 1884 on the ship 'Nevasa', arriving on 8th September, 1884, at Moreton Bay, Queensland.

Their children, in order of birth:

1. 'Maudie' Maud Emily Mary. born in England, Rotherhithe, London, 1883; died Two Mile, Gympie, Queensland 15th August, 1886, aged three and a half years, after two years in Queensland.

2. Rowland Henry Foster, born 1885, Gympie, Queensland; died 2nd September, 1912, aged 27. Lovely obituary in 'Queensland Figaro' 1st October, 1912, Bowen, Queensland. Poet, no issue.

3. Violet Marian (Dolly), born 13th November, 1886 Gympie, Queensland. Married Ken Waugh, Bowen 8th April 1912. Died Brisbane 6th April 1979. Children: Queenie Rosa Gladys Waugh, unmarried; daughter Marjorie Violet Whelan (married Henry 1938; son Andrew Herbert Colin Waugh; daughter Edith Marion, died unmarried in her early twenties.

All of them lived in Ayr, North Queensland until evacuated to Brisbane during the Second World War. Their former address 18 Carter Street, Northgate, Queensland.

4. Andrew Richard, born 27th May, 1888 at The Two Mile, Gympie, Queensland. Died 7th June, 1976, a resident of Wollongong, N.S.W. in the Repatriation Hospital. Concord. Married Betty Blackburn about 1936. No issue.

5. Edith Florence "Queenie", born 30th March, 1890 at The Two Mile, Gympie, Queensland; trained as a nursing sister and died 23rd October, 1936 of a cerebral haemorrhage and heart failure, aged forty-six. Married Dr. Harvey Sylvester Walsh of Brisbane in October 1919. The youngest matron in Queensland to enlist in the First World War, she served in France, Egypt, England and Australia. She and Harvey had two children, a daughter, Rosslyn (Héro), a physiotherapist, (born 30th July, 1923) and a son, Richard, later a doctor at Mt. Gravatt, (born 27th March, 1925).

6. Rupert James, (Jim), born 9th September, 1895, at Ashgrove, Queensland. Married 'Bobbie' Olga Law, 1936 (d. 1938); remarried Merle 1945. One daughter Leigh (Kearney), born 4th June, 1948 and living in 2009 in Melbourne, Victoria. Jim died 23rd April, 1982 at Surfers Paradise, Queensland.

7. Reginald L.L, born 1893, died 29th July, 1898, aged five years.

8. Vivian George, born 1892 and died the same year.

9. Robert Charles, born 28th August, 1901; died in 1920s. One son, Phillip, whereabouts unknown.

10. Leonard Ralph (Pat's father), born 14th April, 1904 at Stafford-on-Kedron, Queensland. He worked in the Commonwealth Bank, rising to the office of manager, and died 9th July, 1972 Manly, New South Wales. He married Mavis Jean Patricia Furner on 26th January, 1932, at St Matthews Church of England, Manly, New South Wales. They had two children: a daughter, Patricia Loris, born 15th February, 1933, and a son, Anthony Leonard, born 1st March, 1938.

Appendix 4: Vital Statistics

Here is a brief overview of the distances covered by Queenie in kilometres and miles, for readers not conversant with the immense distances in Australia and distances from Australia to the overseas countries where she was nursing.

Edith Florence "Queenie" Avenell enlisted in Mackay, North Queensland. Mackay is 993 kilometres, (approximately 603 miles), north of Brisbane, the capital of the State of Queensland. She travelled down to Brisbane on the coastal steamer 'Bombala' from Townsville. Her first letter written from Brisbane in May 1915.

Queenie's mother and brothers were living in Townsville in North Queensland, a sea port. Townsville is north of Mackay and 1384 kilometres north of Brisbane. Innisfail, where she was nursing before enlistment, is further north again. 1,748 kilometres north of Brisbane. Her sister Dolly was living there for most of the war.

Brisbane to Sydney: Distance 581 miles or approximately 950 kilometres south.

Sydney to Melbourne: Queenie travelled by train 908 kilometres south, (approximately 574 miles) to join the troop ship.

Melbourne to Cairo, Egypt by Ship: The 'Mooltan' departed 15th May 1915, arriving in Egypt about 15th June, 1915. This was 13,986 kilometres or 8,690 miles (the modern distance for direct airflight only).

The ship called into Adelaide, the capital of South Australia. The distance from Melbourne to Adelaide is 729 kilometres, and from Adelaide to Perth, the capital of Western Australia 2,708 kilometres. (Distances quoted are by modern highways from Google maps).

Perth to Egypt: 6,992 miles or 11,253 kilometres (modern direct flight distance).

Egypt to Melbourne with the wounded on November, 1915: HT 'Borda' arrived in Melbourne on 13th December, 1915, after travelling 13,986 kilometres or 8,690 miles. (Direct flight distance from www.mapcrow.info)

Melbourne to Egypt on the 'Wandilla': She left Melbourne on 1st January 1916 and arrived Egypt on about 3rd March, 1916: 13,986 km or 8,690 miles (modern direct flight distance info only).

Egypt to Marsailles, France on the HT 'Salta': Departed 29th March, 1916, arrived 6th April.

France to England: A hop, skip and jump across the Channel.

England to Melbourne on the HT 'Euripides': Embarked 21st July, 1917 and arrived Melbourne 18th September, 1917: 10,496 miles, or 16,891 kilometres (modern direct flight distance only).

Her forward travel to Brisbane was on the steamer Tango Maru, a Japanese cargo vessel then on the East Asia to Australia run.

In the census of 1901, Queensland, (which is geographically one of Australia's largest states), had a population of just under half a million. Most living in Brisbane. Of that number 323,436 were born in Australia, 126,159 born in the United Kingdom, 21,174 born in Europe, 13,878 in Asia, 1,500 in New Zealand and 11,577 other. (Aboriginal people were not counted in this census.)

The population of major towns in North Queensland in 1914 were: Townsville 16,900; Charters Towers 4,262; Cairns 5,000; and Mackay 5,300. *(Thank you to Townsville City Librarian, Barbara Mathieson for this information.)*

Smalltown Memorials

No matter how small
every town has one;
Maybe just the obelisk,
a few names inlaid;
More often full-scale granite,
Marble digger (arms reversed),
Long descending lists of dead:
Sometimes not even a town,
A thickening of houses Or
a few unlikely trees
Glimpsed on a back road
Will have one.
1919, 1920:
All over the country; Maybe
a band, slow march, Mayors,
Shire Councils; Relatives
for whom
Print was already
Only print; mates,
Come back, moving
Into unexpected days;
A ring of Fords and sulkies;
The toned-down bit
Of Billy Hughes from an
Ex-recruiting sergeant.
Unveiled;
then seen each day –
Noticed once a year;
And then not always,
Everywhere.
The next bequeathed us
Parks and pools
But something in that first
Demanded stone.

By Geoff Page

This lovely poem is used with the kind permission of Geoff Page and was first published in his poetry book, 'Smalltown Memorials'. UQP 1975.

Bibliography

Bibliography of books used in research or Queenie's letters used in other books:

'Love Letters of an Anzac', by 'Trooper Bluegum', Oliver Hogue.

Published London February 1916 by Melrose Publishing. Search for name of Queenie's then fiancé, Rolland Reid from Christchurch.

'Campaigning with the Fighting 9th, in and out of the line with the Ninth Battalion, A.I.F.' 1914-1919. by Major C.M.Wrench, M.C.' published by Boolarong Press, Queensland, April, 1985. Funded by 9th Battalion Associations. Copy purchased by me from the Gallipoli Barracks Museum, Brisbane. Lee research.

'Letters from an Australian Army Nurse', by Anne Donnell. Angus and Robertson 1920.

Books quoted and also using items and photos from Queenie's Letters.

'Guns and Brooches, Australian Army Nursing from the Boer War to the Gulf War' by Jan Bassett, Oxford University Press, 1992.

(Extract from Chapter Five of her book, summarising the treatment of the Nurses after the First World War): 'They had been given the honorary rank of officers during the War, but paid, of course, as Other Ranks... the few who applied for pensions immediately after the War, owing to illness and incapacity, were only given Other Ranks' pensions". Further, Jan Bassett says, 'More than half of the nurses never married, (most were in their mid-twenties at the beginning of the war). Most were unable to work full-time owing to continuing illnesses, such as malaria from the war. As the nurses' war-time health records were destroyed at the end of the war, this made their applications for War-related Disability Pensions difficult for them to prove'. Many, like Queenie, died young.

According to Jan Bassett, those nurses who did marry, married men who were themselves suffering the continuing effects of their War Service, and the women had to cope with that as well as any children they might have had...Many of the couples were among those who took up the ill-fated Soldier Settler blocks...Those who struggled on in small businesses, such as boarding houses, or private nursing, were wiped out during the Depression of the Thirties. Some Privately funded Trusts had been set up to alleviate the nurses' poverty, but most of the women were too proud to ask for help. The usual amount given out this way was fifteen pounds, (thirty dollars).

Jan continued: 'All Federal Governments continuously ignored representations made to them on behalf of the nurses... Until 1958, forty years after the War, the nurses were still not eligible for treatment in the Repatriation Hospitals and 'adequate lasting care' was finally extended to those suffering from chronic illnesses in 1973! By then, many of the First World War nurses had already died.'

Jan concluded: 'Governments had paid lightly for the First World War nurses' service. Most of the nurses, on the other hand, had paid a heavy price for their wartime experiences.'

'The Forgotten Women' by Mrs. Gwen Robinson of Mt. Gravatt, Brisbane, produced late 1980s with help from Griffith University. Queenie's letters are quoted liberally and her photo sitting in the snow with the young Australian Amputees at Southall is on the front cover.

'Belle on a Broomstick' by Pat Richardson, Gumleaf Press, 1992. Chapter 19. Extra data and chapter on Queenie and the post-war treatment of the WW1 nurses. Quoting Jan Bassett's research.

'Queensland Nurses, Boer War to Vietnam' by Dr. Rupert Goodman. Boolarong Press 1985. Quotes from Queenie's letters and a studio photo of Queenie and Nurse May Tilton taken overseas in World War One, lent by the Tilton family to Dr. Goodman.

The Munster Fusiliers website, www.royalmunsterfusilers.org; information on Lt Alexander Campbell Cunningham, courtesy of James O'Sullivan of Brisbane.

'The Lee Letters from World War One'. Letters home to Maryborough, Qld, from Colonel Harry Lee and his son Major Bill Lee, KIA March 1917. They were emailed to me by Dick Monks, Naremburn, Sydney, with his kind permission to use items if required.

Photos from Queenie's own photo album, with kind permission of her daughter, Rosslyn Héro, née Walsh of Ekebin, Qld.

The Australian War Memorial's database for research and photos, with permission to use their photos. **Also the National Archives data base and 'Trove' the historical site of newspapers.**

Newspaper archives on Trove: The Brisbane Courier, Townsville Daily Bulletin, Cairns Post and The Queenslander.

Plus nearly thirty years of inquiry and help from various people too numerous to mention. Some of the Queenie photos were displayed at Macquarie University, Sydney and restored by the University for their Exhibition of Australian Nurses at War in the 1980s. Thank you to my late mother, Birdie Avenell, for keeping the letters safe at the bottom of her Glory Box, through many moves in the Bank The Avenells being 'travelling Bank Johnnies' or 'travelling schoolies'!

Pat Richardson

HONOUR BOARD
ERECTED BY THE SOLDIERS' CHURCH OF ENGLAND HELP SOCIETY
In the
WAR CHAPEL, ST LUKE'S CHURCH, BRISBANE
In Honour of those members of the
AUSTRALIAN ARMY NURSING SERVICE
Who went from Queensland to serve in the Great War, 1914-1918

WILSON, Grace Margaret
HART, Julia Mary
KEYS, Constance Mabel
PATEN, Eunice Muriel
WILLIAMS, Bertha Mary
ANDREWS, Gertrude Jessie
BUTLER, Ethel Brice
CAMPBELL, Beryl Anderson
CAMPBELL, Eileen Fraser
CROLL, Marion Winfred
DALRYMPLE, Marion
DUNNE, Teresa Josephine
ECHLIN, Gladys Ivy
GIBBON, Beatrice Louisa
HEFFERNAN, Annie Margaret
ISAMBERT, Agnes Kathrine
NILSON, Norma Mabel
PLANT, Armenia Anne
RALSTON, Emily Anne Vardon
SCULLY, May
SNELLING, Louisa
WHIPHAM, Mary Frances
WILSON, Madeline Alice Kendall
AXELSEN, Ida Marie
HARDEN, Catherine Louie
MACDONALD, Flora
McDONNELL, Eveline Florence
WALPOLE, Frances Grace
KENNEDY, Jessie Violet Marion
MACDONALD, Sadie Charlotte
LYON, Stella Zita
LANGFORD, Rose Jane
MacPHERSON, Ada Isabel
* MOWBRAY, Nora Violet
SCOTT, Annie
SORENSEN, Christense
AVENELL, Edith Florence
AITKEN, Violet
BARRON, Ellen
DONNELLY, Charlotte
ELLIS, Dora Leila
GREENAWAY, Sybil
HODGSON, Clara Phoebe
HUXLEY, Margaret Rose
McCLELLAND, Maria Alexandra
ROBSON, Ruth Maughan
SELWYN SMITH, Nita Frances
WALLACE, Florence James
BROWN, Dorothy
CRAVEN, Mary Lee
DE VIS, Gertrude Julia
GRAHAM, Florence
IVERS, Margaretha Dorothy
KEMP, Alice Annie
MARDEN, Emily Clarice Lilla
NAGEL, Amy Louisa
NOTT, Emma Susan
ROW, Ellen Craven
THOMPSON, Beatrice Myra
BEER, Elsie Gertrude
BURNS, Netta
CHRISTENSEN, Victoria Dorothy
DERRER, Mary Jane
FAULKNER, Lavinia Elizabeth
FISHER, Mary Ellen
NICHOLLS, Ruby
POLLOCK, Elsie Jane
RAINE, Christine Annie
SMALLWOOD, Neta May
SMITH, Ada Priscilla
WRIGHT, Hilda Elizabeth
BOWES, Beatrice Clara
CHIDGEY, Ellen
HERBERTSON, Florence

HUDSON, Florence May
MURRAY, Margaret Frances
POLLARD, Ada Rachel
PULLAR, Ellen
THOMAS, Gwladys Mary Helena
TOWNER, Greta Norman
WEBB, Agnes Alice
MOORE, Ida Anna
MITCHELL, Margaret Ellen
McCALMAN, Eileen Jessie
WEBB, Dorothy Frances
GRANT, Elsie Rose
KEMP, Elizabeth Sophy
PARNELL, Louisa Sarah
WRIGHT, Elizabeth Mary
NORTON, Ellen Agnes
ALLAN, Ruth
BATE, Mary Russell
BERRIMAN, Evelyn Rosamond Alberta
CHATAWAY, Mary Esme
HARTE, Catherine
LIVINGSTONE, Mary
NORTON, Annie
PETERSEN, Rosann
WEBB, Mabel
KENNY, Elizabeth
BISHOP, Lily Mary
BRYDON, Jean
DENNIS, Lilian Beatrice
DERRER, Rosine
DOWLING, Marianne
FRANCIS, Sara Stella
GRIFFITHS, Caroline Ross
HARVEY, Margaret Anna
LAWSON, Helen
SEARCH, Dorothy
SMITH, Ida Gertrude Burnett
WILFORD, Isabel Anne
CHEESEMAN, Beatrice Graham
CHAPMAN, Minnie Logie
CLARKE, Evangeline Alace
DODS, Wilhelmina
MANN, Elizabeth
NYE, Gertrude Ada
POWELL, Maude
* WILSON, Myrtle E.

BEAVEN, Stella
BERRY, Charlotte
CHAPMAN, Mary
* CORFIELD, Agnes Beryl
GEARY, Blanche Beatrice
McGRATH, Mary
RAFF, Dorothy
SEXTON, Dora Ethel
GIBBON, Alice May
HENRY, Elizabeth
DICKSON, Edith Beck
TARR, Sarah Jane
MACINTOSH, Isabella Clare
MACINTOSH, Francis Mary
WALKER, Marion Edith
STODDART, Irene
BARNETT, Ethel
SAGAR, Winifred
CUSKELLY, Annie
O'NEILL, Jessie
GOODMAN, Pearl Stella
TOFT, Edith Mary
BIRT, Mary Trevenen
FRANCIS, Ida Grace
CLYDE, Violet Eileen
MORRISON, Maud
QUINN, Lilian Margaret
MORRIS, Sybil Grace
MORGAN-JONES, Vera Hester
BARRON, Janet Ivy
HOMEWOOD, Martha May
GIBSON, Lily Margaret
WARNER, Annie Isabel
FINCH, Jessie
SKYRING, Gertrude May
JESSUP, Eleanor
TARR, Sarah Jane
DICKSON, Edith Beck
LYNCH, Honor
WISEMAN, Mabel Gladys
PROVAN, Annie Harvey
STONE, Amelia Helen
ATHERTON, Rosamond Brenda
COWEN, Kathleen Amy
SHEEN, Edith
SMITH, May Duncan
JONES, Margaret Elizabeth

McLENNAN, Jane
MONCKTON, Catherine
SQUIRE, Daisy Wharton
HARDCASTLE, Lavinia Amelia
IRWIN, Lucy
MORGAN-JONES, Enid Rose
ALTON, Lillian Howard
STIRLING, Violet Jean
DRAKE, Phyllis Clayton
BOWMAN, Isabelle
COOTE, Eva Frances
RIORDAN, Maud
COVES, Beatrice Annie
ANDREWS, Linda Gertrude
LINDSAY, Constance Emma
RELF, Gertrude
BLACK, Catherine Reid
RIGBY, Julia Lyllis
McLEAN, Ella Clow
RICHARDSON, Edith
BARRY, Florence Beatrice
SIM, Annie Grant
KELLAWAY, Sarah
McLEAN, Christina Elizabeth
RITCHIE, Helen
BOWDER, Kate Helen
MacKELLAR, Frances Mary Byron
JAMES-WALLACE, Emily Charlotte
PARKINSON, Olga Gwendolen
PHILLIPS, Rachel Onge
LEYLAND, Beatrice Alice
PAYNE, Winifred
WILSON, Marjorie Jane Gilmore
KAY Flora
FRANCIS, Ruth Sylvia
TOFT, Catherine Ann
MALONEY, May Agnes
JACKSON, Ethel May
MORTON, Gladys Aylward
KEPPEL, Beatrice Emma
LLOYD, Ethel Graham
DAWSON, Helen Frances
BLACK, Elsie Winifred
ROGERS, Muriel Violet
LOOSEMORE, Mary Ann
JESSUP, Eleanor
PHILLIPS, Violet May
CAIRNS, Sarah
SMITH, Dorothy Emma
GRAHAM, Susan May
CAVE, Annie Freda Francis Scully
BROWN, Ruby Davina May
DODD, Alice Maud
MARTIN, Elizabeth
PARKER, Jean

* Died on service.

Editor's note: This honour board was last known to be stored at Anzac House, Brisbane. The editors thank Katelyn Johnson at Anzac House, Brisbane, for her help in finding the Honour Board booklet containing the above nurses' names, which is held in the National Library of Australia. Note that some names were incorrectly spelled on the original honour board; these have been corrected to the spelling shown in the World War One files held by the National Archives of Australia.

St Luke's Church in Charlotte Street, Brisbane, was closed in 1977; it served as an inner city church from 1904, and the church buildings were the headquarters for the Anglican Church Mission. The Romanesque style building is now the premises of the Pancake Manor.

Queenie's Service Friends

A list of the people with whom Queenie served or met while with the Australian Army Nursing Service, from 1915 to 1917, with a letter date on which they are mentioned.

Stawell, Richard Rawdon, Lt. Col
27/5/1915
Donnelly, Charlotte
27/5/1915
Gibson, John Lockhardt, Major 2/6/1915
MacLean, Hector Roth, Major
2/6/1915
Warburton, Thomas, 654
22/6/ 1915
Isaacs, Horatio, 968
22/6/1915
Lee, Harry William (snr)
Lt. Colonel 9th Battalion
(Queenie's uncle)
22/6/15
Tyson, Theresa Adelaide
29/6/1915
Mighell, Norman Rupert, 169 1011
6/7/1915
Gibbon, Beatrice Louise
Honour Board Brisbane
6/7/1915
Birkbeck, Gilbert Major, D.S.O
11/7/1915
Lloyd, Francis Claud, Capt, MC
24/7/1915
Kensett, Walter Francis, Lt
24/7/1915
Fox, Frederick Young, 389
28/8/1915
Williams, Edward Homer, 370
28/8/1915
Hodgson, Clara Phoebe
Honour Board Brisbane
28/8/1915
Lee, Harry William, Major
(Queenie's cousin, KIA France)
20/3/1917
Lascelles, Evelyn Herbert, 357
9/9/1915
Derrer, Mary Jane
Honour Board Brisbane
9/9/1915
Chidgey, Ellen
Honour Board Brisbane
9/9/1915
Cunningham, Alexander Campbell, Lt.
Royal Munster Fusiliers
KIA Gallipoli
14/9/1915
Legge, James Gordon Major General
14/9/1915
Byers, Leslie Ross, 759
21/9/1915
Hobson, William Doyle, 1705
21/9/1915.
Hood, William Frederick, 805
21/9/1915
Reid, Rolland Arthur Lt.
8/10/1915
Grant, Elsie Rose
8/10/1915
Honour Board Brisbane
Warburton, Thomas, 654
8/10/1915
Dunne, Sister Teresa Josephine
Honour Board Brisbane
5/11/1915
Cowton, William Matthew 207
5/11/1915
Argyle, Stanley Seymour Lt. Col
2/3/1916
Cole, Thomas 3790
2/3/1916.
Reid, Lestock, Lt. NZ Army
28/3/1916

Kemp, Sister Alice Annie,
Royal Red Cross
Honour Board Brisbane
28/3/1916
Burrell, Ross, 435
14/5/1916
Earwaker, John George, 2387A
14/5/1916
Conyers, Evelyn Augusta
Matron–in-Chief
29/9/1916
Hogue, Oliver, Major
'Trooper Bluegum'
29/9/1916
Webb, Dorothy Frances
Honour Board Brisbane
29/9/1916
Foxlee, Herbert Walter, Capt.
3/10/1916
Hooper, John, Colonel
3/10/1916
Norris, Herbert Lionel, 2nd Lt.
20/10/1916
Rutledge, Elsie Kathleen
11/11/1916
Crane, Percy Henry Mitchell, Capt.
19/11/1916
Palmer, Charles George,
British ArmySgt
Stepson of Emily Palmer, previously Emily Avenell and Queenie's aunt
(Thank you to Ros Lee of Currumbin for this piece of amazing sleuthing.)
9/11/1916.
Avenell, Andrew,
(Queenie's older brother)
18/1/1917
Chambers, John Cyril, MC, Lt
(Committed suicide during the war, aged 25)
17/2/1917
Oliver, William Douglas 228
6/1/1917
Greer, Geoffrey Harold, 4422
9/2/1917
Thomas, Gwladys Mary Helena
Nurse from Gympie, Queenie's birthplace.
9/2/1917
Trundle, Edwin Francis, Lt.
8/3/1917
Cole, James George, 3143
8/3/1917
Lloyd, Tommy, 10157
18/3/1917
Croker, Charles Raymond, 551
25/3/1917
Kelsey, Augustus Jourdain, Major
25/3/1917.
Jack, Tom Robin, Hon. Capt.
25/3/1917.
Nisbet, Dr Alwyn Tom Hayes, Capt
25/3/1917
Black, Hugh, Lt.
1/4/1917
Francis, Trevor, Capt. MC
1/4/1917
Bernard, Vivian Dalziel, Capt.
1/4/1917
Sellars, Reginald Arthur, Lt.
20/4/1917
Ryan, Charles Snodgrass, Col.
18/4/1917
Avenell, Jim (Queenie's younger brother)
8/5/1917
Falconer, Hugh, Lt.
8/5/1917
Cameron, Colin Ralph, Lt.
15/5/1917
Porter, Simon Fahey, Lt.
15/5/1917
Stevenson, Margaret 'Steve'
15/5/1917
Wilson, Ivor Murray, 733
15/5/1917
Cooper, Ilma Myrtle
10/6/1917.
Phillips, Andrew William, Lt.
9/10/1917
Bond, Sydney Stanna, Capt.
25/10/1917